R. Buckminster Fuller

Education
Automation

Comprehensive Learning for Emergent Humanity

Series Editor Jaime Snyder

LARS MÜLLER PUBLISHERS

Z 01700 2116

Contents

Introduction

We now have aboard our Spaceship Earth more than ample capability to take care of all humanity for all generations to come and to do so at higher standards of living and individual freedom than any humans have thus far experienced or even dreamed of, while in no way endangering the ecological integrity of our planet…. It is also incontrovertibly demonstrable that it is feasible to accomplish this … within ten years while concurrently phasing out all further human use of fossil fuels and atomic energy. We can live handsomely on our annual energy income from the sun and the many modes of its impoundment…. It can only be accomplished by a design revolution which produces so much higher technical performance per each unit of resource invested as to take care of all human needs.

R. Buckminster Fuller, *Education Automation* [1977], pp. 172–73.[1]

I think we have a very brief window of opportunity to deal with climate change … no longer than a decade, at the most.

James Hansen, Director, NASA Goddard Institute for Space Studies; and Adjunct Professor, Earth and Environmental Sciences, Columbia University, in September 2006.

---

1   As Bucky's work often germinated for many years before finding its way into a bound volume, the years given in brackets refer to the year in which the quoted material was originally drafted and/or published rather than the book's publication date; page numbers reference the Lars Müller reprint editions of 2008/10.

In 1961, my grandfather Buckminster Fuller made a presentation to the biennial World Congress of the International Union of Architects (Union Internationale des Architectes, or UIA) in London to call for the launch of a "World Design Science Decade" that would engage architects, architectural schools, and students in a ten-year program to re-design key elements of the world life-support systems, thereby increasing their operating efficiency from 4 to 12 percent, and thus lifting the "high" standard of living enjoyed by 44 percent of humanity to 100 percent using known world resources.[2] His talk sounded a call that reverberated amongst the new generation of students and architects present there, showing up in the architectural journals, interviews, and letters between Bucky and many who would become his associates and partners in the burgeoning movement for a *comprehensive design* revolution.

And it echoed in the subsequent 1963 session of the UIA in Cuba. Bucky was precluded from going to Cuba for the meeting due to Cold War tensions—though he attempted to persuade an acquaintance of his, Undersecretary of State McGeorge Bundy, later National Security Advisor to Presidents Kennedy and Johnson, to allow him to attend by stressing the import of the initiative, it was to no avail. He ultimately presented his further proposal at an international symposium immediately following in Mexico City.

With students and architectural schools inspired around the world, he attempted to coordinate the implementation of a comprehensive game plan from his then recently established headquarters: the World Resources Inventory at Southern Illinois University. Together with young artist and sociologist John McHale, who had just arrived from London to be his point person, they published a series of *World*

---

2   Bucky's calculation of "standard of living" derives from a 1952 analysis he made of world consumption of energy per capita and its relationship to "standard of living" in "developed" and "undeveloped" regions of the world. See R. Buckminster Fuller and John McHale, *World Design Science Decade Document 1* (Carbondale, Ill., 1963), p. 27.

Design Science Decade Documents which included essays and extensive visual mapping of world data, trends, and needs, touching on the "big picture" of every component of the planet's infrastructure.

> Revolution by design and invention is the only revolution tolerable to all men, all societies, and all political systems anywhere. Every nation welcomed the invention of the airplane, and refrigeration. Every nation welcomed and employed the transistor.... All the world, properly informed of the significance of the ... design and invention revolution, will applaud and support the initiative.
>
> *Utopia or Oblivion* [1965], p. 259.

While the impact of these events clearly inspired a new generation of "design revolutionaries," and while the essays from the project showed up in many of Bucky's books of the period, the ten-year project did not spawn the global movement aspired to. Though today we have at our fingertips the kind of computer capability and information technology that we have witnessed facilitate the transformation of powerful ideas into global movements, in 1963 students and architects, spread over the planet, were unable to connect except by traveling to other universities, by preparing work for presentation at periodic meetings, or by correspondence and postal submissions of research. And while Bucky and his team worked diligently to garner state funding for dedicated use of institutional mainframe computers to compile growing bodies of data on global resources, trends, and needs, it was never to materialize.

What makes the "World Design Science Decade" as proposed in 1963 so relevant today is that it may be one of the first "drafts" of a *comprehensive plan* for addressing the "world's problems" and "making the world work for 100% of humanity." With the portfolio of global crises getting bigger each year—nuclear weapons (seemingly ever less secure), systematic environmental destruction, climate change, chronic extreme poverty, failed states, and now this past year the "global financial meltdown"—it becomes starkly evident that what is needed are solutions that are bold, innovative, and, more than anything else, *comprehensive.* They must be comprehensive in addressing both short-term and long-term needs, both immediate symptoms as well as root causes, and, most fundamentally, recognizing the interconnectedness of this web of systemic planetary problems. Solutions that attempt to "solve" certain problems without addressing the others will simply continue to fall short, for they are merely palliatives appearing to move things forward by sweeping messes under the rug that turn out to be someone else's blanket—like sending the waste downstream only to have it foul nearby beaches.

It becomes more and more obvious that we need an immediate and radical re-design of our planet's life-support systems and infrastructure. And yet as powerful as all the networking tools now are, and as broad as the grassroots participation emerging around the planet is, it is clear that the actual implementation of the necessary changes will take many years—a difficult cup of tea to swallow within the quick-fix cultural zeitgeist.

At the same time, the urgency of the matters challenging us is inspiring people, networks, and organizations to action at every level of our society. And there are currently emerging new drafts of *comprehensive plans* for holistically solving the planetary predicament—Lester Brown and the Earth Policy Institute's remarkable *PLAN B 3.0: Mobilizing to Save Civilization* is an outstanding example of one that could not be more comprehensive and do-able with known technology and resources. Another example is Amory Lovins and the Rocky Mountain Institute's *Winning the Oil Endgame: Innovation for Profits, Jobs, and Security.* It is an in-depth, peer-reviewed, Pentagon co-funded, globally-applicable plan for getting the U.S. off of oil within twenty years in a way that revitalizes the very core of the economic engine that is failing. And Rob Hopkins' *The Transition Handbook: From Oil Dependency to Local Resilience* has moved communities, now in the hundreds, around the world to bring comprehensive grassroots self-organized planning to the re-design of local communities. Undoubt-edly there are many other fine examples, but, nevertheless, in the proliferation of new solutions to the vexing challenges facing society, comprehensive thinking and design are still all too rare.

How can we nurture this kind of thinking and these kinds of ap-proaches at all levels of our society, on the front lines of our every-day lives? For it is not the comprehensive plans that give rise to comprehensive thinking, it is comprehensive problem-solving ap-proaches that give rise to such brilliant strategies for addressing the urgent global challenges. So, what is the educational curricu-lum, what is the course of study? What are the fundamental prin-ciples that comprise, inform, and give rise to that kind of thinking? Where are the case studies, what are the rigorous practices of such generalized problem solving and where do we go to learn? Gen-eralized because nature can serve up a wicked curveball and the challenges emerging all around us range from local to regional to national to global, from environment, to health, to food, to energy systems. What is the skill set that prepares someone to grapple with the matter of "re-designing" our global system to serve 100 per-cent of humanity? What are the new paradigms that foster skillful means in this arena?

Bucky saw the answer to this need in the elevation of *design* to a disciplined science founded in awareness of the principles of na-ture's design. He called this approach "comprehensive anticipatory design science":
"comprehensive" because the critical global challenges are systemic;
"anticipatory" because it is much more efficient to prevent heart disease than to cure it; because it is much more cost effective to use water more efficiently than to dig new wells;

"design" because it is much easier to "reform the environment" by inventing and introducing new solutions, like building a bridge, than it is to reform other human beings' behaviors, such as urging them to swim the rapids;

"science" because we need to apply the best practices for establishing facts, gathering information, and identifying principles through experimentation.

So it was with this in mind that I embarked upon what has become a winter ritual, intensively reading Bucky's books to select and prepare the next installment for re-publication. Mid-winter in full throttle I am in the middle of reading five of his books simultaneously. Almost like a horse race, I move back and forth between the volumes to see which one connects most deeply with me, and the concerns of our day. Buoyed along with the sense of possibility in the emergence of a new U.S. president, by the arrival on front and center stage of the notion of a "green economy," by the broad public consensus to get off the use of fossil fuels, and by the dawning recognition that the problems facing our society are an integrated complex which will only be solved boldly and, with a new word seeming to be in vogue, *comprehensively.*

I keep coming back to Bucky's vision of mobilizing young students—now networked globally, now easily accessing the global database of information provided by the Internet, now able to ultra-coordinate with other such students via laptops or smartphones. I think of the great need, as much as any other, to educate and train this next generation of problem-solvers, who are coming up to speed and already joining the implementation. I keep thinking about the young people, or the young in sprit, who are saying, "I want to be a *sustainer* or a *greener,*" who see a career in creating a green economy, who want to develop in themselves the capacity to *solve* the challenging problems facing humanity. I keep sensing an explosion of people thinking "I want to be an Amory Lovins, I want to be a Lester Brown, I want to be a Bucky Fuller—when I grow up." Where can they go? I think too of the "grown-ups" being required to re-invent their careers and lifestyles, not to mention all the semi-retired individuals with the luxury of being able to re-invest more and more free time to engage in the pressing problems of our times.

It was the need to advance the field of comprehensive anticipatory design science and comprehensive design education in general that brought me to select *Ideas and Integrities: A Spontaneous Autobiographical Disclosure* and *Education Automation: Comprehensive Learning for Emergent Humanity* for this year's publications.

As I re-read *Ideas and Integrities,* I found myself continuing to feel it was perhaps the first textbook of "design science"—providing the curriculum that must proliferate and be offered for undergraduate and graduate level programs in design science. It hit me as an under-the-hood immersion in the mechanics of the "Bucky Fuller-mobile" for those who want to know exactly how it works: the principles, the design strategies, the engineering, and its development.

> The specialist in comprehensive design is an emerging synthesis of artist, inventor, mechanic, objective economist and evolutionary strategist.
>
> *Ideas and Integrities* [1950], pp. 232–33.

Though *Ideas and Integrities: A Spontaneous Autobiographical Disclosure* is chock full of raw, hardcore, mind-stretching context and language, rather than being a technical book it may be one of Bucky's most intimate. The subtitle sets the stage, underscored in his background note for chapter 5, "I Figure," calling the volume a "biography of my thought development." The three opening essays include some of his most elegant and accessible self-reflections: "Influences on My Work," "Later Development of My Work," and "Margaret Fuller's Prophecy," an excerpt of the writing of his great aunt Margaret Fuller who had moved him deeply upon his "discovery" of her in the early years of his re-thinking. The other sixteen essays reveal his own evolution, spanning the period from 1942, as he came into his own as a teacher at design schools during the late forties, and his own great explosion onto the world stage in the fifties and early sixties after the invention of the geodesic domes.

Education Automation picks up where *Ideas and Integrities* leaves off. The opening essay "Education Automation: Freeing the Scholar to Return to His Studies," originally published in 1962, derives from a talk Bucky gave on April 22, 1961 in East St. Louis, to the Edwardsville Campus Planning Committee of Southern Illinois University, which was addressing the design of a new campus. SIU in Carbondale, Illinois, was where, only two years earlier, Bucky had become a professor, and he and my grandmother Anne had taken up residence. In the essay he paints a broad canvas, *anticipating* the future of education in one of the early and truly prophetic descriptions of what, almost three decades later, became the information technology revolution via the "two-way TV"—*we* call it the Internet:

I would say, then, that you are faced with a future in which education is going to be number one amongst the great world industries, within which will flourish an educational machine technology that will provide tools such as the individually selected and articulated two-way TV and an intercontinentally networked, documentaries call-up system, operative over any home two-way TV set.

Education Automation [1962], pp. 72–73.

Children will be able to call up any kind of information they want about any subject and get the latest authoritative TV documentary.... The answers to their questions and probings will be *the best information* that is available up to that minute in history.

Education Automation [1962], p. 68.

And yet much more than his description of the coming technology of education, the book answers the question, "education for what?"—a theme broadly expanded upon in numerous essays by Bucky from 1961 to 1976 and added to "Education Automation" in the 1979 book entitled *Buckminster Fuller On Education,* skillfully complied by Peter H. Wagschal and Robert D. Kahn, and upon which this new edition is based. These further essays explore the great need for a truly *comprehensive orientation* in education which never loses sight of the epochal changes unfolding on our planet and the unique role of the individual in steering those evolutionary changes.

Ideas and Integrities and *Education Automation* powerfully intersect at the epicenter of design revolution with their inclusion of material from the original "World Design Science Decade" talks Bucky gave to the International Union of Architects in 1961. Both books exude the paradigm of comprehensive design education. Both books continue to reference the need for a decade-long planetary design initiative. *Education Automation* had been in the editing process for nearly a month and half just before Bucky's July 1961 trip to London to make his presentation to the UIA meeting. Subsequently, at the key "climax" juncture in the manuscript, the beginning of the final thrust, he weaves in a page of his opening UIA presentation there:

> What I now propose is that all the universities around the world be encouraged to invest the next ten years in a continuing problem of *how to make the total world's resources, which now serve only 43 percent, serve 100 percent of humanity through competent complex design science.*
>
> *Education Automation* [1962], p. 100.

For its part, *Ideas and Integrities,* edited by Robert W. Marks and published in 1963, includes two entire chapters (chapter 14, "The Architect as World Planner" and chapter 15, "World Planning") that derive directly from Bucky's presentation on the "World Design Science Decade" at the original July 1961 presentation, and the subsequent follow-up presentation he prepared for the UIA biennial in 1963. In addition, the opening piece, "Influences on My Work" was initially a 1955 letter to John McHale in reply to questions about the genesis of Bucky's work, published in the July 1961 edition of *Architectural Design* at the time of the London UIA congress.

These two new books, in representing the span of Bucky's career from 1942 to 1976, also importantly reflect the evolution of his work as a teacher and educator. As Allegra Fuller Snyder, my mother and Bucky's daughter, pointed out at a lecture this past spring at the Museum of Contemporary Art in Chicago, "In 1949 Bucky took on his first full visiting teacher assignment at the Institute of Design [in Chicago]. The environment was right. It revealed Bucky as an important teacher because he was challenging himself while challenging his students. They challenged each other."

Much of the material in these two books, as would be the case for much of Bucky's later published work, derive from transcripts of his talks. *Ideas and Integrities* comprises the period from those early days in Chicago when the nature of his teaching was characterized by visiting teaching assignments at design, architecture, and art schools, where small groups of students would work with him for a semester with the central focus of "tackling a design problem"—an "autonomous living package," a "failed" prototype for a new kind of structure he would call later a geodesic dome, or subsequently the countless variants of geodesic dome prototypes, testing every kind of geometry, material, and size. Legends abound of his marathon sessions stretching into double-digit hours. *Education Automation* picks up as his work virtually exploded, with geodesic domes cast around the world propelling him onto the world stage; together with an acceleration of published books and press coverage, the audiences grew more frequent and ever larger.

And so it seemed like some kind of confirmation of the readiness, spunk, and appetite of today's student generation that this past spring I learned that the second annual Buckminster Fuller Challenge, a $100,000 prize to the winner of a juried competition for innovative solutions to critical global problems, was awarded to an interdisciplinary team of international students from MIT. Their "Sustainable Personal Mobility and Mobility-on-Demand Systems" project is a breathtaking strategy for urban mobility systems and only underscores the need to engage the next generation in a new *decade* of design revolution. The Buckminster Fuller Challenge jurors published the following statement about their decision: "The winning project is a perfect example of the kind of radical, transformative change that is possible when we reconceive the old ways of doing things and take a systems-based approach to design.… SPM/MoD isn't just about the design of these lightweight, highly efficient, electric vehicles, it is about inserting that technological innovation into the social and cultural environment and designing an intuitive system within which they function."

In 1973, I took a year-and-a-half leave of absence after my first year at college to journey with Bucky on his very heavy pace of traveling the world. By that point he was delivering a major keynote address almost every three days—usually just a couple of hours—to college and "general" audiences commonly in the thousands. Only rarely did we visit a design school, or stay for more than twenty-four hours in a community.

Bucky called his approach to lecturing "thinking out loud" and he disciplined himself "not to think about what he was going to say in advance." As such, all his life's experiences were his reference, including insights gleaned from his design experiments. And while his idiosyncratic engineering-like language could often sound unfamiliar, his message struck a deep chord with audiences of people generally hearing him for the first time—he always elicited a standing ovation.

Having been so "reoriented" by the experience of journeying around the world with him, observing and participating in the kind of work he was engaged in everywhere he went, after it was over it took me a while to digest what it had all been about. What was that chord that resonated? Clearly it was not just designing new inventions, and certainly most in the audience did not aspire to be design scientists. More than anything, more than his specific inventions or his particular ideas, I concluded it was the universal questions he was asking of himself, and everyone else, such as: What can the little individual do that the great institutions of society cannot?

I am sure I am but one of several millions who wonder how much the individual can actually affect the evolutionary processes of his day, while starting only upon his self-accrediting of his own initiative, enterprise and effective transformation capabilities.

Ideas and Integrities [1958], p. 57.

How can a little individual make an impact?

So it could also be true that if your experience actually discerned an industrial gap-closing task that needed your particular experienced attention, and no patron of the task could be discovered who was inherently concerned with such tasks, you might then assume you were being directly challenged by natural evolutionary process with doing something about that gap, which challenge and response were no more mystical than the spontaneous dodging from under a falling tree.

Ideas and Integrities [1958], p. 86.

What are the principles of being effective as an individual? How do I carry on as an individual? What do I do about earning a living if my priority is addressing the "problems" of the world?

The minute you were not concerned with earning a living and really tackled problem after problem that the other fellow was not tackling, there proved to be a wealth of solvable problems. In fact the whole mass of problems that are worth tackling is so great that any average individual who goes into that kind of a paradise wilderness garden ought to make very good progress. If I have made progress that is mildly notable it is only because I walked into a vast, unattended, potential harvest.

Ideas and Integrities [1958], p. 87.

Before it became impractical to do so, after almost every talk crowds of people would find their way backstage and surround Bucky—to have a moment with him, get a book signed, express an idea, or ask him a question. Undoubtedly the most frequently asked question was, "Well Mr. Fuller, I am this or that and a concerned citizen, and what I want to know is, 'What can *I* do to make the world work?'" And he had *one* answer, "You must ask yourself that question; that is what I had to do—that is what the individual is all about; it is not about following some prescription or formula that I can give out."

So what was Bucky's own answer to the question: What can individuals do that the great political, religious, and economic institutions cannot? What was the conclusion for what he often called his life's "experiment" in the efficacy of "individual initiative"? Perhaps the most concise answer is what he asked that we put on his gravestone: "call me *trimtab*." What exactly is "trimtab" and why would he want to be called that?

Something hit me very hard once, thinking about what one little man could do. Think of the *Queen Mary*—the whole ship goes by and then comes the rudder. And there's a tiny thing on the edge of the rudder called a trim-tab. It's a miniature rudder. Just moving that little trim-tab builds a low pressure that pulls the rudder around. Takes almost no effort at all. So I said that the little individual can be a trim-tab. Society thinks it's going right by you, that it's left you altogether. But if you're doing dynamic things mentally, the fact is that you can just put your foot out like that and the whole big ship of state is going to go. So I said, "Call me Trimtab."[3]

The beauty of that little trim tab is that it elegantly *demonstrates* the answer to the question: *What can individuals do* to change the world? And it is precisely that Bucky had found a tested and well-utilized invention, derived from the principles of nature, that can bring confidence in its objective confirmation of what is possible for individuals.

But perhaps more importantly, in these times when we are faced with gargantuan problems and unfathomably large forces invested in their persistence, the trim tab gives us a clue as to *how* little individuals can be effective in the face of such odds. Not only does it demonstrate that a little device *can* steer a very large system, it shows us that the absolutely highest leverage spot in steering the system of that ship is perhaps where one would least expect it, at the very trailing edge of the rudder, at the very back (i.e., stern) of the ship.

Trim tabs also remind us that the front lines of the design revolution are not necessarily in Washington, DC, or in any other global capital; regardless of the merits of a given politician, we are being completely imprudent to act as if we can leave "the mess" to them. The trim tabs of "individual initiative" that drive the necessary changes can turn in the day-to-day actions of each and every one of us.

Think of what we are up against in addressing just one component of one major global challenge: coal's impact on climate change. *Plan*

---

3   R. Buckminster Fuller, page 46 of the transcript of an interview with Barry Farrell for *Playboy*, February 1972.

B 3.0 echoes what many have concluded: we *must* rapidly phase out all coal-fired power plants and replace them with renewable energy! Now that's a big ship to turn—over seven thousand coal plants in the world today, and all the jobs they represent. And when one watches how this is playing out in the U.S., where the political and financial forces fight vigorously any action in that direction, or in China, which at present is building one new coal-fired plant every day, it is very easy to get discouraged without the possibility of proliferating trim tabs.

But, if you look a little closer you find, for example, a dramatic trend toward stopping new coal plant construction; with pressure mounting from all sides against them, and new investment ever more reluctant, there are a growing number of states that are banning or restricting new coal-fired plants. And sitting here writing I look on the Internet for current developments and I find that just weeks ago, it was reported that as a result of a decision by the City of Los Angeles:

> The Intermountain Power Agency (IPA) announced Thursday it has given up plans to build an additional coal-fired unit. Its biggest customer—the city of Los Angeles—signaled its intent July 2 to phase out use of all coal-based electricity by 2020. IPA's expansion project had effectively died in its original iteration when the Los Angeles Department of Water and Power pulled out of the deal in 2007, Reuters reported.[4]

Nations change the world, states change nations, cities and counties changes states, communities change cities and counties, and, all the way at the very tail end of the ship, trim tabs change communities!

4   Tilde Herrera, "L.A.'s Coal Ban Leads to Another Abandoned Power Plant," *Greenbiz.com*, July 13, 2009, http://www.greenbiz.com/blog/2009/07/13/las-coal-ban-leads-another-abandoned-power-plant (accessed August 20, 2009).

This young world is about to take over, to help us design ourselves to make man a success on earth.... We must design
our way to positive effectiveness, and not just be negative
about politicians and what they are doing.

Ideas and Integrities [1962], p. 398.

There have been many revolutions in history. The American Revolution famously began with "the shot heard round the world." There
was Mahatma Gandhi's profoundly powerful *non-violent revolution*
that turned India into a democracy and captured the imagination
of the world community. Perhaps the *design revolution* begins with
the flutter of *trim tabs flapping*—or maybe it is an altogether silent
one, for few in the world would recognize it by that name. Maybe
the announcement by Bucky of his "World Design Science Decade"
project in 1961 was not the epicenter of an earthquake, but a gust
of wind carrying countless airborne seedpods to float off into the
landscape on a gentle summer breeze.

Making the world's totally available resources serve one
hundred percent of an exploding population may only be
accomplished by a *boldly accelerated design evolution* which
adequately increases the present over-all performance per
units of invested resources. This is a task of radical technical
innovation rather than political rationalization.

Ideas and Integrities [1963], p. 339.

When I think of Bucky's advocacy for re-tooling the planet to live
off of our "energy income" rather than our "savings account" of fossil fuels and nuclear energy, which, while in his mind from his earliest writings, really blossomed in the sixties; or when I recall the
"advanced generation" windmill he prototyped with young aeronau-
tical engineer Hans Meyer on an island off the coast of Maine in the
early seventies, it is obvious this "accelerated design evolution"—or
revolution—has come a long way.

That, with sun energy wealth (in one of its many conversion phases) leaking in from a myriad of new sources from which, by any recognized feudal agricultural economic precedent, wealth was not supposed to gush, the astonished discoverer of each latest leak could stand in front of it and fill his back pockets without question of his legal proprietorship to that wealth.

Ideas and Integrities [1942], p. 135.

A half-century later we are witnessing alternative energy front and center on the strategic landscape of current world affairs—a re-design of our world before our very eyes, in a cosmic instant. The *New York Times,* citing a study by the United Nations Environment Program, recently reported that "Global investors spent about $250 billion building new power capacity in 2008, and for the first time the lion's share of that money went to renewable sources."[5] Think of it.

Man now enters the phase of meager yet conscious participation in the anticipatory design undertakings of Nature. This conscious participation itself is changing from an awkward, arbitrary, trial and error ignorance to an intuitively conceived, yet rigorously serviced, disciplined elegance.

Ideas and Integrities [1960], p. 323.

In 2006 I first heard one of the world's leading climatologists, James Hansen of NASA, on television conveying his assessment that we had only ten years left to turn around the climate crisis—in time to avoid a planetary ecological tipping point of no return. This stark wake-up call could only begin to be digested by reflecting upon Bucky's design science decade proposal—which provided some

---

5   James Kanter, "Clean Energy Funding Trumps Fossil Fuels," *New York Times,* June 3, 2009, http://greeninc.blogs.nytimes.com/2009/06/03/clean-energy-funding-trumps-fossil-fuels/ (accessed August 20, 2009).

sense of a possibility that there was a way to turn the ship within ten years. Even though Hansen's "clock" is now down to seven, perhaps we have a running start, since a silent design revolution is well underway. Clearly we do not have the time to wait on some leader to officially launch a comprehensive initiative to address the complex of crises facing us, as John F. Kennedy did in 1961 when he set a goal of putting a man on the moon by the end of the decade. Instead, each of us individual trim tabs will have to declare this project "started," one by one. But with time so short, and the crisis so far beyond just climate change, it is essential we are crystal clear on this "project's" mission.

In the eighties and nineties I was engaged in developing and teaching courses on Bucky's problem-solving approaches in corporate settings. In those days and in the corporate environment, I took note of the fact that the latest *rage* was the "new idea" of "mission statements." For years it seemed like everywhere in the world I went, organizations, institutions, and even individuals had or were developing mission statements. "What is the mission statement of humanity?" "Has one been done?" I wondered. Almost instantly it dawned on me that throughout his career Bucky, through countless statements about "making the world work," had been drafting, developing, and refining just such a statement. And somewhere along the way he had arrived at a version that provides the kind of clarity so desperately needed today. In much the haiku-like form we often associate with mission statements, he proposed:

To make the world work
for 100 % of humanity
in the shortest possible time
through spontaneous cooperation
without ecological offense
or the disadvantage of anyone.

For New Fuller Readers

For those of you reading Bucky for the first time, I offer a few specific tips for your journey through his universe. You may find, with the pulsation from the *macro* to the *micro,* from the *comprehensive* to the *incisive,* that your mind is stretched and turned in a way that is, at first, disorienting. Think of it instead as a re-orientation—a real orientation that can at first be dizzying. Give yourself a lot of time. His books are thinking tools, catalysts for shape-shifting, for leaping far beyond *the box* of normal habitual thought processes. Perhaps a dose-a-day will be your pace, to thoroughly examine and digest the ideas as they come—paying attention to the changes in your own awareness ... daily, weekly, even monthly. Be encouraged: like learning a new language or a new computer program, I trust the current brain researchers would confirm that reading Bucky is just the kind of endeavor that can help us build brain cells and their interconnections.

Bucky also invents new words, or uses common words in ways that are new, precisely because he is attempting to steer clear of the limiting habits of thinking we all inherited. Starting at the age of 32, he made it a discipline, to think carefully about the words he used, resisting the temptation of saying things the way "everyone says them," dispelling the attempt to make them more palatable. For example, he would frequently point out "we still say the words *sunrise* and *sunset,* even though we have known for hundreds of years that the earth revolves around the sun!" In response, someone wrote him suggesting alternatives, *sunsight* and *sunclipse*—which he quickly adopted.

When reading Bucky I find it useful to apply a strategy I learned in foreign language classes: as you begin to converse in the new language let the words pass through without attempting to grasp every one individually. Stick with the continuity, even if it means that on the first time through you miss a number of details. For if you get the continuity, and are able to stay focused on the big picture and the underlying principles, you will glean a sense of the context, even if all the details are not yet clear. And with this general *sense* of what he is saying, you may discover the inspiration that draws you back a second time, to begin progressively examining the details. Bucky suggested this was in fact a principle of universe: there is a fundamental advantage in any problem solving or critical thinking when one "starts with the whole" (or overview), "and then proceeds to the parts" (or details).

A long-time friend and close associate of Bucky's, Don Moore, a gifted systems analyst and engineer, always used to say, "Bucky is the one person I ever met for whom nothing was ever out of context." And for Bucky the context, the way to see clearly our way through the challenges facing humanity, is always by "starting with the whole universe." For Bucky the answers to the problems of our world are all around us in the beautiful design of the universe. And in the end, more than the facts, figures, particular predictions, or solutions he developed, were the underlying principles of universe to which he was pointing. Thank goodness, nature reveals to us the state of the art in design and technology, if we will look.

Jaime Snyder

California, September 2009

Breaking the Shell of Permitted Ignorance

I often make use of two tools of thought that I find important in casting loose from the biases and patterns of yesterday. The first is simply to recognize how powerfully our reflexes are conditioned. For example, the words *up* and *down,* which we all use without much thinking, were invented to accommodate our multimillion-year-old misconception that we lived on a flat world extending laterally to infinity. Since all the perpendiculars to the same plane have to be parallel to one another, they could only go in two directions, up and down. These two words have nothing to do with our spherical planet moving around the sun at 60,000 miles an hour in a Universe where there is no up or down whatsoever. That we still find such expressions appropriate means that we are still thinking in terms of planes that go to infinity: "The four corners of the earth" or "worldwide." This is eminently human. The average person in a lifetime sees less than a millionth of the surface of the earth.

If it really were a plane, stretching omnilaterally to infinity, then there would be infinite room to pollute and infinite resources to replace those already exhausted. Indeed that is the way it seemed in the past, and we are still very much in this frame of mind. Similarly, we still see the sun going down at night and rising in the

November 1972. Originally published in *World* magazine where Fuller served as editor-at-large and wrote a bi-monthly column with the assistance of his associate and friend Michael Ben Eli. Norman Cousins, a long time-friend of Fuller's, started the magazine and served as its editor after thirty years as editor of *Saturday Review,* where he had published of a number of Fuller's pieces.

morning although we have known for 500 years that it is not doing so. Our reflexes can be that much out of gear with what we "know" theoretically. The fact that we "know" a great many "things" does not mean that we are going to behave better.

A second way of thinking, which helps to free one from outdated patterns of thought, has to do with "synergy." This word is not familiar to most people. It means "the behavior of whole systems that cannot be predicted by the behavior of any parts taken separately." That this is not a popular conception can be deduced from the fact that synergy is not a popular word—as I have found by inquiring of 300 university audiences.

A series of important scientific measurements starting in ancient times and later refined observationally by Tycho Brahe and Johannes Kepler disclosed a hitherto unknown mathematical coordination between the planets and the sun. The forces causing this coordination were puzzling since there were no mechanical linkages between the planets, which were all of different sizes and distances from the sun, around which they orbited at different rates. At about the same time, Galileo was measuring rates of free-falling bodies and those sliding on various slopes, and evolving some laws of motion, particularly laws describing the accelerating acceleration of his falling bodies. Newton, excited by all this, sought to discover the mathematical explanations. He reasoned, as had Kepler, that there must be some attractive force operating between the bodies of the solar system. He made the working assumption that a body would persist in a straight line of motion except as affected by other bodies. Newton then calculated what the straight line of the moon's motion would be if Earth were suddenly annihilated. He then measured the rate at which the moon was falling away from the line toward Earth in a given time. He found that the rate of falling corresponded exactly with Galileo's law of falling bodies.

Galileo's accelerating acceleration gave Newton the clue from which he finally evolved his law of mass attraction, to wit: that when the two intercoordinating bodies' masses are multiplied by one another and the distance between them is halved, the attraction is increased fourfold, that is $2^2 = 4$. With certain as yet debatable modifications, Newton's mass-attraction law has since explained all thus far observed macro- and microbehavior of Universe. Yet there is nothing in one of the bodies by itself that tells you it is going to attract or be attracted by another, and that is exactly what is meant by synergy.

The very integrity of our Universe is implicit in synergy, and the fact that the word is popularly unknown shows how relatively ignorant humanity as yet is.

There is a hierarchy of synergies. There is nothing in atoms that predicts the behavior of molecules. There is nothing in molecules per se that predicts the behavior of biological protoplasm. There is nothing in protoplasm per se that predicts the ecological energy-exchanging regenerative coordination of all the living species of our planet.

Going from micro to macro, each more inclusive aspect of Universe is unpredicted by any of its respective subparts taken separately. Universe is a synergy of synergies. It is a corollary of synergy that the known behavior of wholes plus the known behavior of a few of their parts enables discovery of other parts and their behavioral characteristics. In order to really understand what is going on, we have to abandon starting with parts, and we must work instead from the whole to the particulars.

We are all becoming aware of the superb ecological balance whereby the vegetation impounds all the sun's radiation necessary to regenerate all life aboard our planet. In the photosynthetic impoundment of the sun's radiation, the vegetation produces hydrocarbon molecules while giving off gases that would eventually permeate the whole planetary atmosphere if it were not for the mammals who live by these vegetation-produced gases and in turn convert them into the gases necessary to keep the vegetation going. This recirculatory complementation is typical of our whole

Universe. There is nothing that one does that does not affect all others in varying degrees. This, of course, includes all life.

From this point on, we must learn to consider the seriousness of human decisions and actions. But society is still hamstrung by its now obsolete conditioning and inadequate accounting systems.

It is absolutely a priori to everything that I can think about that human beings are born naked and ignorant on board this planet but are given beautiful mental equipment with which, by trial and error, they can gradually learn better how to cope with life. We have not as yet pulled ourselves very far out of that abyss of ignorance. It is important that we realize that we have not. Because of the availability of new communications technology and because we now have a great deal more information, we are supposed to be pulling out very fast, but our reflexes, conditioned by the days of ignorance, are not paying realistic attention to our new information.

We are coming out of a common eggshell of initially permitted ignorance. As with the embryo chick, we were endowed with all the nutriments to nourish us through the period of exclusively subconscious growth. The nutriment for trial and error is exhausted. We are grown. We now know that only our metaphysical mind can and does discover and employ the eternal, weightless, generalized principles governing all Universe transactions. Suddenly our eggshell is broken, and like the chick, we must make good on our own. It must be all or none, and all true to principle.

Education Automation
Freeing the Scholar to Return to His Studies

My feelings about today's meeting with you is, first, that it is a tremendous privilege as a human being to stand with other human beings who are concerned fundamentally and deeply, as you are, with the process and further implementation of education and to be allowed to disclose to you what I think I have discovered regarding education's trending evolutionary needs. I am quite confident that the Southern Illinois University's new Edwardsville Campus studies are uniquely important.

Because President Morris has mentioned it in his introduction of me to this meeting, let me begin with some of my own student experiences at Harvard, for what I have to offer to you today springs from my several educational experiences. I am a New Englander, and I entered Harvard immaturely. I was too puerilely in love with a special, romantic, mythical Harvard of my own conjuring—an Olympian world of super athletes and alluring, grown-up, worldly heroes. I was the fifth generation of a direct line of fathers and their sons attending Harvard College. I arrived there in 1913 before World War I and found myself primarily involved in phases of Harvard that were completely irrelevant to Harvard's educational system. For instance, because I had been quarterback on a preparatory school team whose quarterbacks before me had

April 1961. Originally published by itself in 1962, it derives from a talk Fuller gave on April 22, 1961 in East St. Louis, to the Edwardsville Campus Planning Committee of Southern Illinois University, which was addressing the design of a new campus there.

Figure 1
Dymaxion Airocean World Map

frequently become quarterbacks of the Harvard football team, I had hoped that I too might follow that precedent, but I broke my knee, and that ambition was frustrated. Just before entering college I was painfully jilted in my first schoolboy into-love-falling. Though I had entered Harvard with honor grades I obtained only "good" to "passing" marks in my college work, which I adolescently looked upon as a chore done only to earn the right to live in the Harvard community. But above all, I was confronted with social problems of clubs and so forth. The Harvard clubs played a role in those days very different from today. The problems they generated were solved by the great House system that was inaugurated after World War I. My father died when I was quite young, and though my family was relatively poor I had come to Harvard from a preparatory school for quite well-to-do families. I soon saw that I wasn't going to be included in the clubs as I might have been if I had been very wealthy or had a father looking out for me, for much of the clubs' membership was prearranged by the clubs' graduate committees. I was shockingly surprised by the looming situation. I hadn't anticipated these social developments. I suddenly saw a class system existing in Harvard of which I had never dreamed. I was not aware up to that moment that there was a social class system and that there were different grades of citizens. My thoughts had been idealistically democratic. Some people had good luck and others bad, but not because they were not equal. I considered myself about to be ostracized or compassionately tolerated by the boys I had grown up with. I felt that my social degradation would bring disgrace to my family. If I had gone to another college where I knew no one, it would not have mattered at all to me whether or not I was taken into some society. It was being dropped by all those who had been my friends that hurt, even though I knew that they had almost nothing to do with the selecting. I became panicky about that disintegration of my idealistic Harvard world, went on a pretended "lark," cut classes, and was "fired."

Out of college, I went to work and worked hard. In no time at all, reports went to Harvard that I was a good and able boy and that I really ought to go back to college; so Harvard took me back. However, I was now considered a social maverick, and I saw none of my old friends; it hurt too much. Again I cut classes, spent all my year's allowance, and once more was "fired." After my second "firing" I again worked very hard. If World War I hadn't come along, I am sure the university would have taken me back again, and I am sure I would have been "fired" again. Each time I returned to Harvard I entered a world of gnawing apprehensions, not an educational institution, and that was the problem.

But I did get an education in due and slow course—but an education largely of my own inquiring, experimenting, and self-disciplining. Forty-seven years later, Harvard's Dean Bundy, who was one of Kennedy's White House advisors, invited me to come back to Harvard in 1962, to be the Charles Eliot Norton Professor of Poetry. This is regarded as an honor. The Norton professorship is a one-year appointment. The chair was founded because its donor felt that the university needed to bring in individuals who on their own initiative have long undertaken objective realizations reflecting the wisdom harvested by the educators, which realizations might tend to regenerate the vigor of the university world. Harvard fills this professorship with people who are artists, playwrights, authors, architects, and poets. The word poet in this professorship of poetry is a very general term for a person who *puts things together* in an era of great specialization wherein most people are differentiating or *"taking" things apart.* Demonstrated capability in the integration of ideas is the general qualification for this professorship. I am able to accept the Norton professorship for 1961–62 even though I am a professor on the faculty of Southern Illinois University because I have to be in residence at Harvard only for the months February and March 1962, when I am officially absent from Carbondale.

In the last thirty years of the half century that has passed since my Harvard fiasco, I have been invited as a lecturer, critic, or experimental seminarist to visit 106 universities around the world, and many of them quite frequently. I have had appointments, for instance, to Princeton University nine times, starting back in 1929, M.I.T. eight times, North Carolina State eight times, University of Michigan five times, Cornell University four times, and that's the way it has gone. There have been many revisits, and all of my visits have been entirely a consequence of their inviting me to come. I developed a self-discipline long ago regarding exploration on the science, technology, philosophic, and economic frontiers which requires that I must not spend any time asking people to listen to me or to look at what I may be doing. If, however, what I am discovering seems to be of interest to others and they ask me what it is that I am working on, I will tell them. I am quite confident that if in the evolutionary processes we deliberately attempt direct personal exploitation of the economic advantages accruing to our personal scientific explorations, we inadvertently become preoccupied and prejudiced with the item we have to sell and are no longer free to explore scientifically with a wholesome intellectual integrity.

By my own rules, I may not profess any special preoccupation or capability. I am a random element. Considering these self-imposed conditions, I am happy that I have been asked back to the universities, and I am happy that several of them have seen fit to give me an honorary degree. At Washington University, where I had been a one-month visiting critic and lecturer for four successive years, the university gave me a degree of Doctor of Science, "with all the rights and privileges thereonto attached." I feel that this was not an exclusively honorary degree; the circumstances were akin to those of a doctoral candidate. My degree was voted unanimously by the university faculty as a direct consequence of my campus work. Though I have degrees awarded by other leading universities under similar working or earned circumstances as

Doctor of Arts, Doctor of Design, and Doctor of Humanities, I am confident that I am not professionally classifiable. I do know, however, from personal experience that there is nothing even mildly extraordinary about me except that I think I am durable and inquisitive in a comprehensive pattern. I have learned much; but I don't *know* very much; but what I have learned, I have learned by trial and error. And I have great confidence in the meager store of wisdom that I have secured.

As a consequence of my university visiting, I have had about two thousand students who have worked with me in different parts of the world. As I go around the world I find these students active and doing well. When I arrive in New Delhi, Nairobi, or Beirut I find that the students know that I am coming. They are waiting for me with programs they have arranged, and I am able to assess the effect of the kind of learning and communication we have shared. I am confident that the students I have worked with are trending to become strong citizens around the world. That, I find, is one of the best tests of the validity of whatever communicable wisdom may have harvested and disbursed from my experiences.

My experience is now world-around. During one-third of a century of experimental work, I have been operating on the philosophic premise that all thoughts and all experiences can be translated much farther than just into words and abstract thought patterns. I saw that they can be translated into patterns which may be realized in various *physical* projections—by which we can alter the physical environment itself and thereby induce other people to subconsciously alter their ecological patterning. My own conclusion is that we have been given the capability to alter and accelerate the evolutionary transformation of the a priori physical environment—that is, to participate objectively, directly, and consciously in universal evolution—and I assume that the great, complex integrity of omnicoordinate and interaccommodative yet periodically unique and nonsimultaneously cooperative generalized principles, and their myriad of special case realizations, all of which we speak of as Universe and may think intuitively of as God, is an intellectual invention system which counts on our employing these capabilities. If we do not do so consciously, events will transpire so that we function subconsciously in the inexorable evolutionary transformations.

As a consequence of our having the faculty to apprehend patterns external to ourselves and the capability of altering those patterns, interesting changes in the conscious relationship of human beings to Universe are now multiplyingly in evidence. Unlike any of the other living species, human beings have succeeded both consciously and subconsciously in greatly altering their fundamental ecological patterning. None of the other living species have altered their ecological patterning. All the species other than human beings are distinguishable throughout geologic and biologic history by their approximately unaltered ecological patterning. In the last half-century, we have graduated from a local twelve-mile-radius daily domain into a world-around multithousand-miles-radius daily domain, as a consequence of our ability to alter our own ecological patterning.

I have for a third of a century been convinced that thoughts must be translated into patterns that can be articulated out of the organized capabilities of human beings and that these patterns, which can be translated from our thoughts into physical actions, then become utterly impersonal facilities that begin, when adopted in emergencies, to change the relative advantage of human beings spontaneously and subconsciously with respect to their total environment. It is a philosophic requirement of my comprehensive working hypotheses that the intellectually projected tools which result in new ecological patternings must give human beings consciously appreciable, advantage increase. My experience shows that these impersonal tools tend to eliminate many of the errors of conceptioning that people who have not translated their thoughts into experimental physical undertakings have heretofore imposed upon one another as inherited *conventional* thoughts and misinterpretations of their respective experiences—misconceptions which they have hopefully and lovingly gone on relaying for ages from one generation to the next.

I am convinced that humanity is characterized by extraordinary love for its new life and yet has been misinforming its new life to such an extent that the new life is continually at a greater disadvantage than it would be if abandoned in the wilderness by the parents. For an instance of misconception extension there is my own case. I was born in 1895. The airplane was invented when I was nine years old. Up to the time I was nine years old, the idea that man could fly was held to be preposterous, and anybody could tell you so. My own boyhood attempts to make flying machines were considered wasted time. I have lived deeply into the period when flying is no longer impossible, but nonetheless a period in which the supremely ruling social conventions and economic dogma have continued to presuppose a nonflying-person ecology.

My daughter was not born into the kind of a world that I was; so she doesn't have to struggle to sustain the validity of the particular set of spontaneously logical conceptions that were pronounced "impossible" in my day, nor need she deal with the seemingly illogical concepts that the older life thought to be "evident" and "obvious" in my day. The new life is continually born into a set of conditions where it is easier for it to acquire more accurate information, generated almost entirely outside of family life and folklore, regarding what is going on in human affairs and in nature in general; and, therefore, the new life has the advantage of much more unshaken intellectual courage with respect to the total experiences than have its as yet living elders who have had to overcome these errors, but who retain deep-rooted delusively conditioned, subconscious reflexes.

As a startling consequence of the as-yet prevalent and almost total misconceptioning regarding traditional education, both formal and informal, I have heard the following problem discussed among leading scientists. A serious question arises when a university student demonstrates extraordinary capability in science as judged by our present academic criteria. The exceptionally high-ranking student has completed graduate work, and if enabled to develop further there is high probability that the student might be able to make important contributions to science and therethrough to society. There are funds available to foster the super education of this promising individual, but first there is a decision to be made concerning resources much more important than money. This person is going to have to be associated with some of the senior, proven, living scientists—some of the very rare great people—in order for the latter to find out whether the neophyte is a real front-rank scientist. The neophyte is going to have to be given the opportunity to grow in that association with the proven great one. Therefore, society is going to have to risk wasting some of the preciously meager remaining lifetime of its proven, really high-powered intellects, should the candidate fail to demonstrate exceptional capability. Whether that risk is warranted becomes the strategic question. As a consequence, the kind of examination procedure that our science foundations and other science leaders have developed is one in which they explore to discover whether the capable students are able to unlearn everything they have learned, because experience has shown that that is what they are going to have to do if they are to become front-rank scientists. The frontiers of science are such that almost every morning many of our hypotheses of yesterday are found inadequate or in error. So great is the frontier acceleration that now in a year of such events much of yesterday's conceptioning becomes obsolete.

I said I started a number of years ago exploring for ways in which individuals could employ their experience analytically to reorganize patterns around them by design of impersonal tools. To be effective, this reorganization must incorporate the latest knowledge gained by humanity. It also should make it an increasingly facile matter for the new life to apprehend what is going on. It should eliminate the necessity of new life asking questions of people who don't know the answers, thereby avoiding cluttering up the new minds with bad answers which would soon have to be discarded. I felt that the evolving inventory of information "decontaminated" through competent design might be "piped" right into the environment of the home. Please remember my philosophy is one which had always to be translated into inanimate artifacts. My self-discipline ruled that it would be all right for me to talk after I had translated my philosophy and thoughts into actions and artifacts, but I must never talk about the thoughts until I have developed a physical invention—not a social reform.

That is the philosophy I evolved in 1927, when at thirty-two I began my own thinking. I have been operating since then on the 1927 premises, looking exploratorily for tasks that needed to be done, which would, when done, provide tool complexes that would begin to operate inanimately at higher advantage for the new life. I am the opposite of a reformer; I am what I call a new former. The new form must be spontaneously complementary to the innate faculties and capabilities of life. I am quite confident that humanity is born with its total intellectual capability already on inventory and that human beings do not add anything to any other human beings in the way of faculties and capacities. What usually happens in the educational process is that the faculties are dulled, overloaded, stuffed, and paralyzed, so that by the time that most people are mature they have lost use of many of their innate capabilities. My long-time hope is that we may soon begin to realize what we are doing and may alter the "education" process in such a way as only to help the new life to demonstrate some of its very powerful innate capabilities.

I went to the World Affairs Conference in Colorado last week. At the meeting were many important individuals—the ambassadors of Ghana, Nigeria, and so forth. Also participating were economists, sociologists, and scientists, and among them was a Yale scientist, Dr. Omar Moore. Dr. Omar Moore, you may recall, was reported on in *Time* magazine last year. At Yale University in the Child Study Clinic, he began to be suspicious that there were drives in human beings other than those of *fear* and *longing* which have been the assumed *fundamental* drives. He developed a hypothetical working assumption that there was a drive of the new life to *demonstrate competence,* and began working with his own child when she was two and one-half years old. He took an electric typewriter and colored the keys to correspond with the touch system. He then colored his child's fingernails to correspond with the keys each finger should operate. He had a hidden electric key, and when she didn't match the correct finger to the typewriter key the circuit was not closed. When she put the correctly colored finger on it the key worked, and quickly she learned to match her fingers to the proper keys. Every time she touched a key with the proper finger, not only did it print on the paper, but a big letter also came up in a window. By the time the child was three she was typing swiftly with the touch system the stories that were generated in her imagination. She seemed to find it just as easy to communicate this way as by talking. Dr. Moore's community and a number of his colleagues who happened to live in the same little town became fascinated, and began working experimentally with their children. There was a wave of excitement. These men say they used to like to get the children to bed early so they could have the evening to themselves, but now they hate to have the children go to bed early because everyone is so excited and stimulated by what this new life is demonstrating in capacity and capability. These are just some of the inklings corroborating what I am saying regarding very powerful faculties born in the human being which, if given the opportunity, may very readily regenerate to higher advantage for other people.

As a consequence of my kind of technically objective philosophy, I have had wide and copious experiences and firsthand practice in mechanics and structures. I am an engineer by tutorial work with one of our country's leading engineers of the 1920s; I am capable in the general world of physics and mildly capable in the world of chemistry; I am a mathematical explorer. I have been able to translate many of my philosophies into physical inventions in gap areas where there have been no previously recognized functions whatsoever—where people have not thought of the problems as being soluble by some device, but soluble only by social procedure reforms. As a consequence, I have developed quite a number of unprecedented devices and structures. At the present there are almost two thousand of my geodesic domes in forty countries around the world.[6] All of those structures are of an unprecedented type. They were patentable in the countries around the world because they were unprecedented and were not included in structural engineering theory and therefore were true inventions. They enclose environments at about 1 percent of the invested weight of resources of comparable volume enclosed by conventional structures with which you are familiar. They had to meet the hurricanes, the snow loads, and so forth. My structures are also earthquake proof; most of their comparable conventional counterparts are not. I have found it possible to do much more with less.

I have been able to demonstrate that there are important patterns to be employed by human beings and that there are inherently available ways of thinking which are simple and logical. My exploration into mathematics has disclosed extraordinary and comprehensive mathematical patternings of nature. I am quite confident that I have discovered the coordinate system employed by nature itself, in contradistinction to the arbitrarily adopted "x, y, z" system which science employs and by virtue of which it translates its calculus through analytical geometry into informations which can be used technically.

---

6   According to Fuller, by 1983 there were over 300,000 geodesic domes built throughout the world. Fuller's "Basic Biography," March 1983.

All my discourse to you thus far has been given as an introduction in which I have related examples of my experiences and their derived philosophy. I gave you this in the hope of earning your credit for whatever I may be able to say exploratorily regarding what I think is going to happen in the immediate, educational-process future with which you are specifically concerned.

I am a student of trends. I am confident that my overall trend data is good and that my forecasting capability has proven reliable. From 1938 to 1940, I was technical editor on *Fortune* magazine—at least that was my function; they don't have that title on their masthead. In the period 1936 to 1938, I had been assistant to the director of research of the Phelps Dodge Corporation, which was the third largest copper corporation in the world. For Phelps Dodge, and indirectly for the World Copper Committee, I developed some comprehensive world economic-trend patternings in order to learn what the overall trend in world industry might be and what copper's functioning within it might be. Many of my trend prognostications were fulfilled and acknowledged by Phelps Dodge. These world economic-trend patterns were of renewed value when my suggested main theme and research were adopted by *Fortune* magazine in February 1940 for the subject of their tenth anniversary issue. I had to employ a number of the accounting staff of Time, Inc., to carry out the large-scale work, because the subject was "U.S.A. and the World." We went into all that was known at that time about the economic patternings of people on Earth, the industrial equation, and the posture of the United States in that picture. That issue of *Fortune* was so successful that it went into three reprintings and took *Fortune* from the red into the black side of the ledger.

Incidentally, the relative world economic advantage of the United States as of 1940 was so prodigious that it was astounding. Our relative advantage today is anything but that. It was not that we had about 75 percent of all the world's industrial products but that we had the confidence of much of the world that democracy was unbeatably the most favorable political system. We have been frittering away an enormously high credit that the world spontaneously extended to us. Our world credit has deteriorated. The ambitions of the world's people and the needs of humanity have not been wisely serviced by us in the last score of years, 1940 to 1960. Because national, foreign, and domestic policies of government and business failed to heed such world-trend studies and continued to revert to the pre-air-age conventions and concepts of independent local sovereignties and business anarchy we have lost that world credit of our initiative and integrity. It can be won back, but only through the integrity of education.

Out of my general world-pattern-trend studies there now comes strong evidence that nothing is going to be quite so surprising or abrupt in the forward history of humanity as the forward evolution in the educational processes. People think that it is exciting to consider going to the moon and that such a trip will be a revolutionary affair. Of course it will. We may have all kinds of world warring and so forth, and these are spectacular. But in our shifting times the world tends to think of its educational processes as well-developed and quite reliable, needing only expansion, therefore not subject to excitingly important changes, and therefore the antithesis of news-making moonshots.

As a consequence of this public attitude there is the prevalent tendency of politicians to feel that they are going to be secure of their return to office by virtue of getting all they can for their constituents in the way of "educational facilities" as a well-established and familiar commodity. It is very characteristic of all those undertakings that when the politicians think about education they immediately begin to think about buildings and apparatus. There is a conventional picture or concept of school that is very powerful in most people's minds, and I think a great surprise is coming. I don't think that what is going to happen in education is apprehended or anticipated at all by the political states. I know that

Figure 2
Mercator Projection World Map

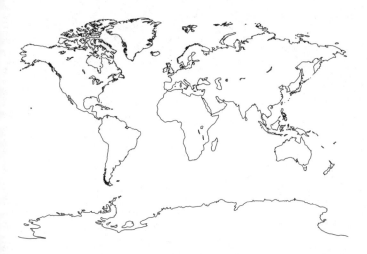

there is awareness of coming change amongst the forward thinkers of the educational ranks, but, I feel, even they will be astonished at the magnitude of the transformation about to take place
in the educational processes.

I have put up on the wall my Dymaxion Airocean World
Map.[7] I am sure it doesn't look familiar to you. Some of you may
have seen it—there was an early version of it published in *Life*
magazine in 1943—but it was a little different from the one on the
wall. The same spectrum colors were used, but it was a slightly
different geometrical pattern. If we were to go around this school
building and look at the world maps on its walls, we would probably see several Mercator maps Figure 2. Sometimes we would see

7   In 1952, Fuller working with Shoji Sadao, published the first edition of the ico-
sahedral version of his world map (fig. 1), now increasingly referred to by cartogra-
phers as the "Fuller Projection" world map, using the convention commonly used for
world map projections such as the Mercator, Robinson, and Peters Projections. His
first world map published in the March 1, 1943 issue of *Life*, was based on the cubo-
octahedron. For more information, see: http://bfi.org/our_programs/who_is_buckminster_
fuller/design_science/dymaxion_map/the_fuller_projection_map.

Figure 3

Icosahedron

Figure 4

Azimuthal or Gnomonic
Projection Method

Figure 5

Conic
Projection Method

Figure 6

Mercator
Projection Method

U.N. maps. These projections do not show the Antarctic. The U.N. map is a north-polar azimuthal. It is greatly distorted in the Southern Hemisphere and has no Antarctic and, therefore, misses a very large continent. You are probably thinking that my world map is "interesting," but that you would rather have a "regular" map. Our concept of the "regular" map is typical of our mental fixation in the educational processes. On the Mercator, as you know, the North Pole area is so completely distorted that it is seemingly thousands of miles from Greenland to Alaska. Many thousands of miles are indicated at the top edge of the Mercator between

North Pole points one mile apart—completely misinforming. The Mercator map tends to show Europe and Asia split in two, so that "never the twain shall meet," as Kipling said. The Americas are in the center. The "tops" of the continents don't join together at all, and there are the great open blank spaces of the Arctic and Antarctic. Those were very good maps for the era of sailing when the Arctic and Antarctic were unexplored "infinities."

My world map which you are looking at on the wall has strange 60-degree angle-edge patterns. If you will cut out along the gray edges and bring them together, you will find that the map will make an icosahedron Figure 3—that is, a "solid" faced with twenty equilateral triangles. If you will compare its data and graphic patterning with that of a globe, you won't find any fault with it at all. It will seem to be saying just what the world globe says. The shapes of the land masses are correct; there is no visible distortion of the relative shapes or relative sizes of its geographical features. This is a pretty good map because no other projection will do that. The polar azimuthals Figure 4, the polyconics Figure 5, and the Mercators Figure 6—the prime "regular" types—all have a very great distortion in them. My map does not. I discovered a topological transformation between spheres and planes. I was able to get a United States patent—the first United States patent ever granted on a method of projection. Though my map is hung in many distinguished people's offices, the fact is that it is not hung in the schools. The big map companies go right on turning out the maps that, as far as I am concerned, are extremely distorted, misinforming, and obsolete.

Let me point out next that when you transfer the projected data from the surface of a sphere to a plane you have to break open the spherical skin in order to "peel" it. There will be various angular cuts in the periphery of the skin when it is layed out flat, just as when you take the skin off an animal. The openings along the edge are called sinuses. The sinuses on my map all occur in the water. None of the cuts go into the land. Therefore, I am able to take all of the data off the earth globe and make it accurately available to you in the flat. You can't see around the world globe; in fact you can only *read* one fourth of the globe at any one time; so it is good now that you can see all the data at once in the flat without visible distortion or breaks in the continental contours. My map in effect shows one world-island in one world-ocean. We have been aware that only one quarter of the earth's surface is dry land, but we have not acknowledged that there is one ocean. We speak of at least three oceans. When this one-world-island is rotated as you now see it displayed on the wall, you say, "I see the United States now and it is 'right side up.'" The fact is, there is no such orientation in Universe as "right side up"; so what you mean is your habitual way of looking at things. This map can be cut into triangles. You can put them together in many different ways. The arrangement on the wall just happens to be a preferred way of putting the triangles together. I watched the head of the mathematics department of a leading university observe his children putting a similar map together on the floor. He said, "No, darlings, you have it upside down. You are supposed to have the United States so that it's up." The children were quite right, of course, and the head of the math department was wrong. He was demonstrating a debilitating fixation on the *conventional* map. I assert that this disclosure is typical of our entire educational process, of the kinds of conceptual fixations we have that are debilitating to the older people in considering the needs of the young peoples' world and the enormous new potentials that can be integrated to the advantage of the young.

Four percent of humanity is for the moment in South America. One percent is in Central America, 7 percent in North America—a total of 12 percent in the combined Americas.[8] From anywhere in the United States, as only my map shows, I can fly the shortest

8   The United Nations reports that in 2009 Latin America comprises 8.5 percent and North America 5 percent of world population. *Population Prospects: The 2008 Revision; Highlights* (New York, 2008).

great-circle routes to reach 84 percent of humanity without flying either over the Atlantic or Pacific oceans. This is not the pattern that we have been thinking about with our Mercator maps. With them we think in terms of *necessarily* crossing the Atlantic and Pacific, going back to the great sailing era days and the great significance of the ports of embarkation and debarkation and of the great tonnages being shipped between them. In terms of air transportation, however, *this*—the one-world-island land mass on the Fuller map—becomes the airstrip of the world which is most significant, and this airstrip is oriented at 90 degrees to the Mercator stretch-out. This is the appropriate world communications and transport orientation for the present moment. Older people still think they must go to New York from St. Louis to go to Europe, but that really is not the right way to go. This is the right way to go—northern great-circle routes. That is why Chicago, despite New York and San Francisco being very attractive places to embark from, is the most heavily used airport in America.[9]

People generally think "go north go cold, so south go warm." That is a fixation which is also not true. On my map, the spectrum colors are used. I use these for the mean low temperatures for the year. The mean highs are about the same everywhere; that is, in eastern Siberia it gets as hot in the summer as it gets in mid-continent Africa on certain days. The major climatic differences between the various parts of the world are in the extremes of cold, or the "lows," not in the "highs," or heats. The hottest days in Brazil and India are about the same as the hottest days in eastern Siberia and Alaska. The cold pole of the Northern Hemisphere is in eastern Siberia. The cold pole for the Southern Hemisphere happens to coincide geographically with the south pole of the earth's rotational axis. You see on my map how the colors change

---

9   At present, Hartsfield-Jackson Atlanta International Airport accounts for the most passengers boarded; Kennedy International in New York accounts for the greatest number of passengers boarding international flights, according to Bureau of Transportation Statistics data for 2008. http://www.bts.gov/press_releases/2009/bts019_09/html/bts019_09.html#table_04 (accessed August 23, 2009).

from blue to green to yellow to red. Blue is coldest. Red is hottest. We find that the red masses of Africa, South America, and South Asia belong to the Northern Hemisphere's color-spectrum bull's-eye. The world thermal map in effect makes a "target" pattern, with the spectrum color-ring zones primarily coordinate in terms of the Northern Hemisphere. There is also a small secondary color-spectrum temperature-zone bull's-eye associated with the Southern Hemisphere's cold pole, but it is much smaller than the Northern. It has green in the southern tip of South America and some yellow and red. There is a little yellow and mild red that belongs to the Southern Hemisphere in Australia. Only the southern-most tips of Australia, Africa, and South America are primarily affected by the south cold pole. The rest of the world temperature-patterning relates to the north cold pole. Ninety-nine percent of the world's population lives at present in the north cold pole's weather domain.

In Europe you will find that the spectrum of thermal-zone lines runs east and west, contrary to the "go north go cold, go south go warm" fixation. The hottest place in Europe is Spain, and Europe gets colder as we go east, not north. Napoleon, thinking as everybody does, that when you stay in your home latitude you will have about the same temperature and weather, went east into Russia prepared to find conditions similar to his home conditions. He was licked by the cold. He dissipated enormous amounts of energy against the cold, the great negative of energy. You would think that by the time Hitler came along people would have learned something about this thermal map. They had not, and Hitler, too, went east into Russia. He was licked logistically by the unexpected magnitude of cold. For an instance, he did not have the right locomotive greases for the temperatures that his army ran into. As a consequence of the thermal ignorance, his forces were not properly supplied, and their hitting power was dissipated by the cold. The cold turned Hitler's tide. This was due, then, to the fact that the concept of go north to cold is wrong. This is ignorance again typical of the educational fallacies. I am sure that parents are still going to teach this geographical error to their children, but the fact is that where 76 percent of humanity now exists it is "go east, go cold" and in only 24 percent of the world's land is "go north go cold, go south go warm" true.

We can also look at the colors on the map and compare them with the colors of people's skins. The map temperature colors have to do with the radiation, the inhibition of energy from the sun. As we get into the great cold areas, the skin gets very, very white. People have to hibernate a great deal of the time. In other parts of the world they could be naked with a great deal of sun. The colors of the map are related, then, also to the color of pigmentation of the skins. This has something to do with the solar system and nothing to do with some mysterious "different kinds of tribes" around the faces of the earth. If there are any special differences in the shapes of noses or heights of people, it has to do very much with the long isolation of people and the developing of certain amounts of hybridism in relation to adapting to special local conditions. There are some dark-skinned people up in the Arctic among the Eskimos, and they are people who came there relatively recently from the tropics and Japan, from the darker regions, by water. They are water people. That is enough discussion of the map.

I was asked to speak in Japan a month ago by Governor Azuma of Tokyo, now the world's largest city. Tokyo is a province as well as a city. There are so many people they make it a province with a governor. He asked me to speak to his planners and council about planning for Tokyo's future. I pointed out to him that in most of the universities I visit we get into town planning. The planning game is always operative in the terms of a "San Francisco plan," a "St. Louis plan," "East St. Louis plan," or "Lack of East St. Louis plan." Planning as taught is a target-town discipline. I pointed out that this is no longer an adequate way of looking at the planning problem. We will have to find out first what is happening to humanity in the big world pattern—where it is going—find out what the world's probable and comprehensive changes are in order to understand what you've got to plan for any particular city. I recalled that at Massachusetts Institute of Technology in 1949 the planning department was working on the greater Boston plan. It turned out in the end that despite M.I.T.'s exclusively local considerations, what was really happening to Boston in an entirely unplanned manner was that it was becoming a vast clover leaf for a continental highway delivery system of our national hitting power from the entire complex of industry in the eastern United States focused to the northeastern most "jump off" point of the United States, should there be a hot war. They were really rubbing out old Boston to make room for the military highway system. The preoccupation with Boston was nonsense. M.I.T.'s planners ought at least to have been talking about the larger highway system and much better about the big world traffic patterns that are developing and how Boston might possibly function in them. They should have been asking: "What does Boston have that is going to make it of any importance whatsoever tomorrow?" If you can find out what that is, then you will know how not to be surprised by what happens and you will know how to accommodate what is going to happen. Boston, despite much "planning," is in 1961 one of the United States' prime depressed areas while many nonplanned areas are booming.

There are many big patternings transcendental to humanity's general apprehension which are developing gradually into inevitable recognition in the world. One of the biggest *inevitables* concerns world-humanity ecology and discloses the fact that at present people are completely mistaken in fundamental ecological thinking regarding themselves. They tend to think of themselves as a tree, as having roots. Up to World War I, the "good citizen" was the person who "owned his own home"—a very well-known expression even today. People also think of themselves as natives of one country, of one state, of one town, of one homestead. There are two ways in which life tends to be ecologically successful. One is in a static way as a tree. Trees do have roots, and the pine tree as a species "goes around the world" by having its seeds airborne. The pine moves around the world not as an individual tree but by successive generation relaying and airborne regenerations. Human beings are one of the species that do not have roots and are successful by virtue of their dynamic ability to advance and retreat. We are mobile. Our little legs are very small, and we don't cover much territory compared, for example, with a sea gull. We, therefore, have tended to think of ourselves as being more like a tree simply because of the diminutive size of our daily peregrinations. We found it difficult to get along without close association with other people, and up to World War I, with minor exceptions, remained essentially within a very small geographical pattern—that is, the territory or even the towns in which we were born.

The average distance viewed from the top of a tree to the horizon is fourteen miles. To the horizon and back is, then, about twenty-eight miles. One learns in the Army that twenty-five miles is a very good day's hike. When our movement was only by legs very few people ever went all the way to the horizon. They stayed pretty well within the sight of one another. They had to develop very static rules and mores—customs that would be acceptable to the dullest and rudest while seeing a whole lot of one another. Our popular political and social and economic reflexing developed along those lines, and holds vigorously today. The concepts of real estate, or of banking and mortgage economics, are theoretically predicated upon people staying "put." Our whole political system is based on the assumption that people belong to special pieces of land, as do trees, and they are expected to stay there. They have political representatives from each geographical point. "Where is your home?" or "Where do you come from?" are considered logical questions.

In the last two United States censuses there were some surprises for those static-roots concepts. The census seven years ago showed that every year an average of 20 percent of America moved out of town. When I was a little boy, we had two "moving days" each year in the New England towns, and I understand they had them in the western towns, too. About twice a year people made new lease contracts for the next year's rented quarters. The economic successes of the previous year began to show up; so some people moved to worse quarters and some to better quarters—a kind of economic musical chairs. What we learned from our census seven years ago was that every year 20 percent of America moved *out of town.* They didn't just move around and play musical chairs in town as they used to forty years ago. This meant that, in effect, *every five years all of America moved out of town.* The preliminary figures are coming in from the last census of a year and a half ago, and they show that America is now moving out of town every three years. This is quite an acceleration. Within six years America has accelerated from moving out of town every five years to moving out of town *every three years.* We are not staying put at all. We are in an enormous pattern of comprehensive acceleration which, however, like the hands of a clock, is a subvisible rate of motion. If you or any one else can say, "I have never moved out of town," it is because many such as I move out of town every week or month.

Up to World War I most people had only their feet to get around on; a relatively few people had horses. People all around the world—as has been measured with pedometers by a number of the world's armies—averaged 1,300 miles walking, per capita per annum. This is an average which includes the extremes ranging from the postman to the bedridden invalid. Up to World War I those 1,300 walked miles constituted the limit of humanity's possible ecological sweepout—1,300 miles per annum local to-and-froing. As we entered World War I, Americans were getting from one place to another by some means other than their own legs, a distance of approximately 350 miles a year. They were walking 1,300 and riding 350 by trains, horses, or ships; so they were predominately a walking device, and the mechanical addition though notable as yet added only 25 percent. As we came out of World War I, the phenomena of mobilization—the production of trucks, cars, railway rolling stock, and ships in enormous numbers—suddenly brought about a change in America. By 1919 the average American was moving annually 1,600 miles by mechanical vehicles and continuing to walk the 1,300 as well. For the first time in all history, humanity had suddenly increased its ecological sweepout. The wolves don't increase their ecological sweepout; the gulls don't; the crabs don't. But human beings suddenly occupied a bigger territory, ergo, entered into an entirely new kind of "life." Since that time, the miles per capita per annum of human beings have increased enormously not only in America by Americans but all around the world by almost all the world's peoples.

As we entered World War II, in America we were up to 4,000 mechanized miles per capita per annum in addition to the constant 1,300 miles of annual footsteps. However, special categories of people were doing much more. The average American housewife was doing 10,000, salesmen 30,000, the air hostess 100,000 miles per year. At the present moment we are sweeping-out an average of approximately 9,000 miles per capita per annum. Also, at the present moment there are more Americans at all times outside of the United States—actually in world travel—than the number of people populating the United States when it was founded. We are swiftly approaching a complete annual world sweepout by all world people. By the end of this coming decade a person will be able to take a commercial plane, catching it at the nearest commercial airport, and after breakfast reach any part of the world, do a day's work, and be home for dinner. We will be in a "one town world" in a realistic way.

We talk about ourselves as a *nation*. We are not a nation and never have been. Russia has about 150 *nations*. These nations are people who have been isolated remotely from other nations for thousands of years and have become enormously hybrid in relation to their special success in their special geographical areas. This hybridism is temporary, a consequence of the areas and environments, and not of there being fundamentally different species of people around Earth. How does that evolutionary hybridism come about in the Darwinian mechanics? It does not come about through physical transformation in any one individual in that person's lifetime but through changes in successive generations. For instance, certain birds live in an area where they get out of the water something vital that is their main food. Suddenly the water begins to recede in that area, and the birds have to dig even more deeply into the mud for food. The birds that don't have long beaks can't reach the food, and though the longer-beakers could relay food to the shorter-beakers there is not time enough for them to do so and survive. Thus only the long-beakers survive; the shorter-beakers starve and become extinct. This means that when the long-beakers want to get married there are only long-beakers around; so they begin to inbreed long-beakers, for the probability is that two similar hybrids will produce a similar hybrid. This is the way the hybrids develop in any special area. That is why *nations* require many generations of utter isolation to develop unique national characteristics.

What is happening on our world during recent milleniums is that there has been a net western motion of humanity. In the very early days there was a comprehensive eastern motion of humanity drifting with the tides and the prevailing winds, but for the last eight or ten thousand years, there has been a net comprehensive motion westward heading into the prevailing winds. Implemented with the swiftly improving tools which came out of the seafaring evolution, people moved on the high sea, and with the kinds of technology and economics which the sea developed these people became great structural and geographic and mathematical and commercial and piscatorial pattern masters. Off of the early raft came the shelter, which had to be a very light hut structure, else the raft would sink. Gradually some raft people took their sheep up on the land, and they didn't have to carry the structure with them for their housing, because they could remember the structural pattern. They could get saplings where they went and weave them together as a large upside-down basket from the remembered pattern. Then they could take the skins of the goats and sheep which they tended and ate, and make them into covers. Consequently, they were able to survive in very cold areas. The 150 nations of Russia today are people who went westward from the seashores of the Orient into the vast Asiatic hinterland many cold milleniums ago.

As people began to learn with catamarans how to design ships that would sail into the wind they went westward into the prevailing winds. These westbound seafaring people kept coming together westwardly along the Indian Ocean coasts with the hinterland wandering peoples coming down finally out of the hills from their cold hibernating westward peregrinations. Finally, these coastal convergences of westward-bound overseas and overland peoples occur in a very big way historically as the westbound into-the-winds overland tribes and the westward-bound into-the-wind sailors came together in Mesopotamia and next on the Mediterranean shores. The Ionian Greeks are a crossbred product of the people coming both from over the vast inland reaches of the Eurasian continent and from over the Indian Ocean waters having first hit the eastern coast of Africa and then boated northward "down" the Nile to the Mediterranean or navigated with camels, "ocean schooners," across Mesopotamia and Arabia to the Mediterranean. Thereafter we have a continual pouring together of these westbound land and sea people along the northern and southern shores of the Mediterranean—flowing eventually into Europe. Ultimately, many overland and overseas westbound tribes crossbreeding, crossbreeding, crossbreeding, completely absorb the earlier static European nations of long-pocketed hybrids. The westward migrating overland and sea people were continually developing more comprehensive adaptability out of the complex of hybrid-demonstrated functions through invention of better and better tools to replace those integral body-articulated functions. Then we have the western jump completely across the Atlantic to America. The people who first came to the eastern shores of America from Europe were already extremely crossbred—the French, English, and Germans. America's population today is, then, a westbound, complexedly crossbreeding one—not a nation.

Very interestingly, I heard at the World Affairs Conference in Boulder four years ago a leading English journalist get up and say, "We might as well face it, the white race is about to be exterminated by the black and the yellow." I asked him what color white is, and he said, "Well, what color is it?" I told him it is all colors. What we call the white man is really a pink man. We pink-whites are the products of Arabic-Indian sailors and overland Vandals, Goths, Mongols, etc., moving along the waterfronts, running into the local hybrids, and crossbreeding with them over a great period of years. We are not only a crossbred people in America but also an advanced state of reversion to a generalized type which becomes the pink-white, all-colors person—the antithesis of local national hybrid types. We are simply the westernmost frontier of crossbreeding people trending toward a generalized world-person type, and very *rapidly,* evolutionarily speaking. You will have to realize that this is so in preparing your new educational processes in which you will have all kinds of problems arising from false fixations of society in respect to a supposedly persisting and valid nationalism, which in reality scarcely exists anywhere anymore and not at all in America except amongst the Indians.

The headache of a president of a great university is today probably the next biggest headache to that of a quasi-nation's president. Take the problem of how to get the funds for this enormous educational undertaking. You educators are uniquely associated with people who are well educated and who have a great feeling of responsibility toward the new life. There is an enormous task to be done, and the budget gets to be formidable. How do you raise the funds? The now world-populated state universities have to keep raising funds from a political base which as constituted is inherently static, operating exclusively in terms of Illinois or Ohio or whichever state it may be.

The point is that we—both as individuals and as society—are quite rapidly uprooting ourselves. We never were trees and never had roots, but due to shortsightedness we believed blindly and behaved as though we did. Today we are extraordinarily mobile. In this last election, 10 percent of the national electorate were unable to vote because they hadn't been in their new places long enough. The accelerating mobility curve that I just gave you indicates that by the next election 25 percent of America will not be able to vote due to recentness of moving, and in the following election possibly less than the majority will be able to vote. We are simply going to have to change our political basis. We are now at the point where the concept of our geographically based representation—which assumes that it realistically represents the *human* beings—is no longer valid. The political machine alone will continue to stay local. It sees the people as statically local. So those who are politically ambitious just stay put while society moves on, and, therefore, the static politicians become invisible to the swiftly moving body politic, which cannot keep track of their static machinations since society does not stay long enough in any one place to be effective in reviewing the local political initiations. The political machines soon will have no one to challenge realistically their existence validity except the local newspapers, whose purely local political news becomes progressively of less interest to a world-mobilizing society.

Comprehensively, the world is going from a Newtonian static norm to an Einsteinian all-motion norm. That is the biggest thing that is happening at this moment in history. We are becoming "quick" and the graveyards of the dead become progressively less logical. I would say, then, that your educational planners are going to have your worst headaches because you will have political machines that are less and less visible to the people because the people are more and more mobile. You will have to be serving the children of the mobile people who really, in a sense, don't have a base, and you will have to justify it with very hard-boiled local political exploitation. I am not particularly optimistic about the kind of results you are going to get. Therefore, when I begin to talk about the educational revolution ahead I see that the old system is probably going to become paralyzed. That is why your headache will get worse and worse until nature just evolutes and makes enormous emergency adjustments. President Morris, I not only recognize that your job is fabulously challenging, I recognize you as an extraordinarily able man. Yet I see that you are going to have a harder and harder time, and nobody could care more than you do about the good results you might get. What I am saying, then, is realistic. It is also going to be obvious to you, I am sure, that the kind of changes I will talk about next are probably going to have to take place.

We know that our world population is increasing incomprehensibly swiftly. There are enormous numbers to be educated. We are going to develop very new attitudes about our crossbreeding and our reversion to universal pigmentation. That is going to be slow, but it is going to be a great and inevitable event. In the end we are going to recognize that there are no different species of living human beings, and we will get over that kind of color class-distinction.

The big question is how are we, as educators, going to handle the enormous increase in the new life. How do we make available to these new students what we have been able to discover fairly accurately about Universe and the way it is operating? How are we going to be able to get to them the true net value won blindly through the long tradition of ignorant dedications and hard-won lessons of all the unknown parents and all the other invisibly heroic people who have given hopefully to the new life, such as, for instance, the fabulous heritage of humanity's stoic capacity to carry on despite immense hardships?

The new life needs to be inspired with the realization that it has all kinds of new advantages that have been gained through great dedications of unknown, unsung heroes of intellectual exploration and great intuitively faithful integrities of people groping in the dark. Unless the new life is highly appreciative of those who have gone before, it won't be able to take effective advantage of its heritage. It will not be as regenerated and inspired as it might be if it appreciated the comprehensive love invested in that heritage.

The old political way of looking at things is such that the political machine says we first must get a "schoolhouse" for our constituents, and it must look like Harvard University, or it must be Georgian and a whole big pile of it. "We see that the rich kids went to school in automobiles; so let's get beautiful buses for our kids." "Harvard and Yale have long had football; our school is going to have football." There is nothing children used to have that they are not going to "get" from their politicians, who, above all, know best how to exploit the inferiority complex which they understand so well as handed down from the ages and ages of 99 percent have-not-ness of humanity. There is a sort of class inferiority amelioration battle that goes on with the politicos in seeking the favor of their constituents to get into or back into office, and little if any attention is paid to the real educational problems at hand.

In thinking about these problems, I have thought a lot about what I have learned that may be useful as proven by experiments in my own self-disciplining. I have met some powerful thinkers. I met Dr. Einstein. I wrote three chapters in a book about Dr. Einstein, and my publishers said that they wouldn't publish it because I wasn't on the list of people who understood Einstein. I asked them to send the typescript to Einstein, and they did. He then said he approved of it—that I had interpreted him properly—and so the chapters did get published. When Einstein approved of my typescript he asked me to come and meet him and talk about my book. I am quite confident that I can say with authority that Einstein, when he wanted to study, didn't sit in the middle of a schoolroom. That is probably the poorest place he could have gone to study. When individuals are really thinking, they are tremendously isolated. They may manage to isolate themselves in Grand Central Station, but it is *despite* the environment rather than because of it. The place to study is not in a schoolroom.

Parents quite clearly love their children; that is a safe general observation. We don't say parents send their children to school to get rid of them. The fact is, however, that it is very convenient for parents, in order to be able to clean the house for the family, to have the children out of the way for a little while. The little red schoolhouse was not entirely motivated by educational ambitions.

There is also a general baby-sitting function which is called school. While the children are being "baby-sat," they might as well be given something to read. We find that they get along pretty well with the game of "reading"; so we give them more to read, and we add writing and arithmetic. Very seriously, much of what goes on in our schools is strictly related to social experiences, and that is fine—that's good for the kids. But I would say we are going to add much more in the very near future by taking advantage of the children's ability to show us what they need.

I have taken photographs of my grandchildren looking at television. Without consideration of the "value," the actual concentration of children on the message which is coming to them is fabulous. They really "latch on." Given the chance to get accurate, logical, and lucid information at the time when they want and need to get it, they will go after it and inhibit it in a most effective manner. I am quite certain that we are soon going to begin to do the following. At our universities we will take the people who are the faculty leaders in research or in teaching. We are not going to ask them to give the same lectures over and over each year from their curriculum cards, finding themselves confronted with another roomful of people and asking themselves, "What was it I said last year?" This is a routine which deadens the faculty member. We are going to select, instead, the people who are authorities on various subjects—the people who are most respected by others within their respective departments and fields. They will give their basic lecture course just once to a group of human beings, including both the experts in their own subject and bright children and adults without special training in their field. These lectures will be recorded as Southern Illinois University did my last lecture series of fifty-two hours in October 1960. They will make moving-picture footage of the lectures as well as hi-fi tape recording. Then the professors and their faculty associates will listen to the recordings time and again.

"What you say is very good," the professor's associates may comment, "but we have heard you say it a little better at other times." The professor then dubs in a better statement. Thus begins complete reworking of the tape, cleaned up, and cleaned up some more, as in the moving-picture cutting, and new illustrative "footage" will be added on. The whole of a university department will work on improving the message and conceptioning of a picture for many months, sometimes for years. The graduate students who want to be present in the university and who also qualify to be with the scholars who have great powers and intellectual capability, together with the faculty, may spend a year getting a documentary ready. They will not even depend upon the diction of the original lecturer, because the diction of that person may be very inadequate to the professor's really fundamental conceptioning and information, which should be superb. A professor's knowledge may be very great, but a scholar may be a poor lecturer because of poor speaking habits or false teeth. Another voice will take over the task of getting the professor's exact words across. Others will gradually process the tape and moving-picture footage, using communications specialists, psychologists, etc.

For instance, I am quite certain that some day we will take a subject such as Einstein's theory of relativity, and with the "Einstein" of the subject and his colleagues working on it for a year, we will finally get it reduced down to what is "net" in the subject and enthusiastically approved by the "Einstein" who gave the original lecture. What is net will become communicated so well that any child can turn on a documentary device, a TV, and get the Einstein lucidity of thinking and get it quickly and firmly. I am quite sure that we are going to get research and development laboratories of education where the faculty will become producers of extraordinary moving-picture documentaries. That is going to be the big, new educational trend.

The documentaries will be distributed by various means. One of the ways by which I am sure they will be distributed eventually has very much to do with an important evolution in communications history which will take a little describing. First, I point out to you that since the inauguration of the United States and adoption of its Constitution some very severe alterations have happened in the evolution of democracy's stimulation and response patterning and the velocity and frequency rates of that patterning's event-transformations.

At the time we founded our country, men were elected in small local areas out of communities wherein all the people were familiar with all the faces. Everybody knew Mr. Forbes or whatever his name was, and they trusted him and elected him to represent them in their federal assembly meetings. These "well-known" representatives of the eighteenth and nineteenth centuries had to go to the Congress by foot or horse, for those were the means of travel. For instance, they went from some place in Massachusetts to Philadelphia or Washington, wherever the Congress was convening, and it took them a week or so to get there. They stopped along the way, meeting many friends and other folk and finding out what the aspirations of the different people's localities were. Let us hypothetically consider how they conferred at their

Congress on their individual needs and requirements; how they found certain things that were of general pertinence to all of them and found some things that were relevant only to individual areas. While they were meeting they received a letter from France, and they were very excited because France, who had helped them in the Revolution, now critically needed some help from the new United States of America. They talked about what they might do about that letter. All of these men then went back by foot or horse to their different homes and conferred face to face with their townspeople. They told their constituents what they had found out about the various things, and they said: "Here's a letter from France; this is what the various representatives at the Congress thought about it—what do you think about it?" Then they went back to the central meeting place again and acted on that letter and other pertinent matters in view of their direct knowledge of their constituents' thoughts and ambitions. The term of office that we gave representatives was predicated upon this ecological pattern of on-foot and horseback traveling. It took about four years to complete the two trips just outlined to effect a basic democratic stimulation and response cycle. The velocity rates of stimulation and response were in a one-to-one correspondence.

Suddenly new industrial technology made scientific harvesting available through invention. Lincoln became the first "wired" president—the first head of a state to be able to talk directly by telegraph to his generals at the front. This was the first time generals no longer needed to be sovereignly autonomous, because now the head of state became practically available for the highest policy decisions right at the front. World War I brought in the radio, and in World War II, for the first time, the admirals at sea were hooked up directly to Washington. They didn't need the autonomy they had to have when they took the fleet away for a year with no way to communicate with the president other than by a messenger sailing ship. Now "we the people" have radio and TV, and we obtain world-around event information from the telegraph, newspaper, and broadcast. With world-around news broadcast to us in seconds, there is no way we can respond directly to their problem-content stimuli.

We no longer have the one-to-one velocity and frequency correspondence between stimulation and response that we had in the early formative days of the United States. We now have enormous numbers of stimulations and no way to say effectively what we think about them or what we would like to do about each of them. By the time that presidential voting comes around every four years we have accumulated ten thousand unvented, world-around emanating stimulations, and usually we are no longer in the same town with the representatives that we previously elected.

Automobiles move through the streets with pictures of political candidates' faces on their sides, and we try to pick out the candidates whom we think least offensive. We rarely know them or whether we may trust them. So we vote superficially for the "least offensive" ones, depending primarily on the major party selections. That is about the best we can do.

Because all this is so, those now doing the representing, wishing to be returned to office, wish to know what people are thinking about all the important issues. So the surveys of public opinion have developed, and congressional investigations of many phenomena have increased. We have to have a kind of anticipatory political reconnaissance going on all the time. Even then, when the elected officials come in they know that it is only as the result of indirect effects of total psychological moods; so they pay little attention to any specific "mandates," and they begin to work right away on the psychological culturing of their next election. They are not really sure that there are any true mandates. They don't really know what the people think. That is one large reason why democracy is in great trouble today, because of the vacillation and compromise arising from the lack of one-to-one correspondence between stimulation and response of the electorate. The Communists and dictatorships scoff at democracy—saying it doesn't work.

I am sure that democracy is inherently more powerful and capable and appropriate to human needs than any other form of government, but it needs proper updated implementation to a one-to-one velocity correspondence in respect to each and every stimulation-and-response, and then democracy can work—magnificently.

I have talked to you about solving problems by design competence instead of by political reform. It is possible to get one-to-one correspondence of action and reaction without political revolution, warfare, and reform. I find it possible today with very short electromagnetic waves to make small reflectors by which modulated signals can be beamed. After World War II, we began to beam our TV messages from city to city. One reason television didn't get going before World War II was because of the difficulty in distributing signals over long distances from central sources on long waves or mildly short waves. We were working on coaxial cables between cities, but during the war we found new short ranges of electromagnetic frequencies. We worked practically with very much higher frequencies, very much shorter wave lengths. We found that we could beam these short waves from city to city. Television programs are brought into the small city now by beam from a few big cities and then *rebroadcast* locally to the home sets. That is the existing TV distribution pattern. My invention finds it is now possible to utilize the local TV masts in any community in a new way. Going up to, say, 200, 300, or 400 feet and looking down on a community you see the houses individually in the middle of their respective land plots. Therefore, with a few high masts having a number of tiny massers, lassers, or reflectors, each beam aimed accurately at a specific house, the entire community could be directly "hooked up" by beams, instead of being broadcast to. This means a great energy saving, for less than 1 percent of the omnidirectionally *broadcast* pattern ever hits a receiving antenna. The beaming makes for very sharp, clear, frequency-modulated signals.

In the beaming system, you also have a reflector at the house that picks up the signal. It corresponds directly to the one on the mast and is aimed right back to the specific beaming cup on the mast from which it is receiving. This means that with beam casting you are able to send individual messages to each of those houses. There is a direct, fixed, wireless connection, an actual direct linkage to individuals; and it works in both directions. Therefore, the receiving individual can beam back, "I don't like it." He may and can say "yes" or "no." This "yes" or "no" is the basis of a binary mathematical system, and immediately brings in the "language" of the modern electronic computers. With two-way TV, constant referendum of democracy will be manifest, and democracy will become the most practical form of industrial and space-age government by all people, for all people.

It will be possible not only for an individual to say, "I don't like it," on his two-way TV but he can also beam-dial (without having to know mathematics), "I want number so and so." It is also possible with this kind of two-way TV linkage with individuals' homes to send out many different programs simultaneously; in fact, as many as there are two-way beamed-up receiving sets and programs. It would be possible to have large central storages of documentaries—great libraries. A child could call for a special program information locally over the TV set.

With two-way TV we will develop selecting dials for the children which will not be primarily an alphabetical but a visual *species* and *chronological category* selecting device with secondary alphabetical subdivisions. Children will be able to call up any kind of information they want about any subject and get the latest authoritative TV documentary, the production of which I have already described to you. The answers to their questions and probings will be *the best information* that is available up to that minute in history.

All this will bring a profound change in education. We will stop training individuals to be "teachers." Much of the educational system today is aimed at answering: "How am I going to survive?

How am I going to get a job? I must earn a living." That is the priority item under which we are working all the time—the idea of *having to earn a living.* That problem of "how are we going to earn a living?" is going to go out the historical window, forever, in the next decade, and education is going to be disembarrassed of the unseen "practical" priority bogeyman. Education will then be concerned primarily with exploring to discover not only more about Universe and its history but about what Universe is trying to do, about why human beings are part of it, and about how can, and may humanity best function in universal evolution.

Automation is with us. There is no question about it. Automation was inevitable to intellect. Intellect was found to differentiate out experience continually and to articulate and develop new tools to do physically repeated tasks. People are now no longer *essential* as workers in the fabulously complex industrial equation. Marx's *worker* is soon to become utterly obsolete. Automation is coming in Russia just as it is here. The word *worker* describing people as muscle-and-reflex machines will not have its current 1961 meaning a decade hence. Therefore, if we are no longer essential as workers, we ask: "How can we live? How do we acquire the money or credits with which to purchase what we need or what we want that is available beyond immediate needs?" At the present time we are making all kinds of economic pretenses at covering up this overwhelming automation problem because we don't realize adequately the larger significance of the truly fundamental change that is taking place in respect to people-in-universe. As automation advanced, people began to create secondary or nonproductive jobs to make themselves look busy so that they could rationalize a necessity for themselves by virtue of which they could "earn" their living. Take all of our bankers, for example. They are all fixtures; they don't have anything to do that a counting machine couldn't do; a punch-button box would suffice. They have no basic banking authority whatsoever today. They do not loan you their own wealth. They loan you your own wealth.

But people have a sense of vanity and have to invent these things that make them look important.

I am trying to keep at the realities with you. Approximately total automation is coming. People will be essential to the industrial equation but not as workers. People are going to be utterly essential as consumers—what I call *regenerative consumers,* however, not just swill pails.

The vast industrial complex undertakings and associated capital investments are today so enormous and take so long to inaugurate that they require concomitantly rapid regenerative economics to support them. The enterprise must pay off very rapidly in order to be able to refund itself and obtain the economic advantage to inaugurate solution of the next task with still higher technical advantage. In that regenerative cycle of events, the more consumers there are the more the costs are divided and the lower the individual prices. The higher the frequency of the consuming, the more quickly the capital cost can be refunded, and the sooner the system is ready for the next wave of better technology. So people are essential to the industrial equation as consumers—as regenerative consumers, critical consumers, people who tasting want to taste better and who viewing realize what they view can be accomplished more efficiently and more interestingly. The consumer thus becomes a highly critical regenerative function, requiring an educational system that fosters the consumer's regenerative capacity and capability.

At present, world economics is such that Russia and China work under an integrated socialist planning in competition with our literally disorganized economic world (for our antitrust laws will not permit organization on a comprehensive basis). The Communists have high efficiency advantage because of their authoritarianism. We have very little centralized authority, save in "defense." The Communists now have the industrial equation, too, in large scale, and soon complete automation will be with them. They are very much aware of the fact that the more customers there are, the more successful the operation will be, because the unit costs are progressively lower. This is why the Soviets were historically lucky in getting China as customers. They would like also to have, exclusively, India and Africa as customers. If Russia acquires the most customers, we will not be able to compete. They will always have the lower costs on any given level of technology. We are going to have to meet this possibility and meet it vigorously, swiftly, and intelligently. Within the next decade, if we survive at all as an organized set of crossbreeding people on the American continent it will be because we will have suddenly developed a completely new attitude on all these matters. In case you are apprehensive that social and political economics are to be so laggard as to impede your advanced educational programming, it is well to remember that the comprehensive world economics are going to force vast economic reforms of industries and nations, which incidentally will require utter modernization of the educational processes in order to be able to compete and survive.

Every time we educate a person, we as educators have a regenerative experience, and we ought to learn from that experience how to do it much better the next time. The more educated our population, the more effective it becomes as an integral of regenerative consumer individuals. We are going to have to invest in our whole population to accelerate its consumer regeneration. We are going to be completely unemployed as muscle-working machines. *We as economic society are going to have to pay our whole population to go to school and pay it to stay at school.* That is, we are going to have to put our whole population into the educational process and get *everybody* realistically literate in many directions. Quite clearly, *the new political word* is going to be *investment*. It is not going to be dole, or socialism, or the idea of people hanging around in bread lines. The new popular *regenerative investment* idea is actually that of making people more familiar with the patterns of Universe, that is, with what people have learned about Universe to date, and that of getting everybody intercommunicative at ever higher levels of literacy. People are then going to stay in the education process. They are going to populate ever increasing numbers of research laboratories and universities.

As we now disemploy people as muscle and reflex machines, the one area where employment is gaining abnormally fast is the research and development area. Research and development are a part of the educational process itself. We are going to have to invest in our people and make available to them participation in the great educational process of research and development in order to learn more. When we learn more, we are able to do more with our given opportunities. We can rate federally paid-for education as a high return, mutual benefit investment. When we plant a seed and give it the opportunity to grow, its fruits pay us back many fold. Humanity is going to "improve" rapidly in the same way by new federally underwritten educational "seeding" by new tools and processes.

Our educational processes are in fact the upcoming major world industry. This is *it;* this is the essence of today's educational facilities meeting. You are caught in that new educational upward draughting process. The cost of education will be funded regeneratively right out of earnings of the technology, the industrial equation, because we can only afford to reinvest continually in humanity's ability to go back and turn out a better job. As a result of the new educational processes our consuming costs will be progressively lower as we also gain ever higher performance per units of invested resources, which means that our wealth actually will be increasing at all times rather than "exhausted by spending." It is the "capability" wealth that really counts. It is very good that there is an international competitive system now operating, otherwise people would tend to stagnate, particularly in large group undertakings. They would otherwise be afraid to venture in this great intellectual integrity regeneration.

I would say, then, that you are faced with a future in which education is going to be number one amongst the great world industries, within which will flourish an educational machine technology that will provide tools such as the individually selected and articulated two-way TV and an intercontinentally networked, documentaries call-up system, operative over any home two-way TV set.

The new educational technology will probably provide also an invention of mine called the Geoscope—a large 200-foot diameter (or more) lightweight geodesic sphere hung hoveringly at 100 feet above midcampus by approximately invisible cables from three remote masts. This giant sphere is a miniature earth. Its entire exterior and interior surfaces will be covered with closely packed electric bulbs, each with variable intensity controls. The lighting of the bulbs is scanningly controlled through an electric computer. The number of the bulbs and their minimum distance of 100 feet from viewing eyes, either at the center of the sphere or on the ground outside and below the sphere, will produce the visual effect and resolution of a fine-screen halftone cut or that of an excellent television-tube picture. The 200-foot Geoscope will cost about $15 million.[10] It will make possible communication of phenomena that are not at present communicable to our conceptual understanding. There are many motion patterns such as those of the hands of the clock or of the solar system planets or of the molecules of gas in a pneumatic ball or of atoms or the earth's annual weather that cannot be seen or comprehended by the human eye and brain relay and are therefore inadequately comprehended and dealt with by the human mind.

The Geoscope may be illuminated to picture the earth and the motion of its complete cloud-cover history for years run off on its surface in minutes so that we may comprehend the cyclic patterning and predict. The complete census-by-census of world

---

10 While one wonders what dramatic advances in information technology might yield in cost savings, $15 million in 1960, adjusted for inflation using the Consumer Price Index (CPI), is $108 million in 2009 dollars. http://www.bls.gov/data/inflation_calculator. htm (accessed July 15, 2009).

population history changes could be run off in minutes, giving a clear picture of the demological patterning and its clear trending. The total history of transportation and of world resource discovery, development, distribution, and redistribution could become comprehendible to the human mind, which would thus be able to forecast and plan in vastly greater magnitude than heretofore. The consequences of various world plans could be computed and projected. All world data would be dynamically viewable and picturable and relayable by radio to all the world, so that common consideration in a most educated manner of all world problems by all world people would become a practical event.

The universities are going to be wonderful places. Scholars will stay there for a long, long time—the rest of their lives—while they are developing more and more knowledge about the whole experience of humanity. All people will be going around the world in due process as everyday routine search and exploration, and the world-experiencing patterning will be everywhere—all students from everywhere all over the world. That is all part of the new pattern that is rushing upon us. We will accelerate as rapidly into "yesterday" through archaeology as we do into "tomorrow." Archaeology both on land and under the seas will flourish equally with astronautics.

As I came to this meeting today, I wasn't surprised by East St. Louis, because I have been here many times. I have been traveling around the world so much that seeing East St. Louis once again reminds me that right in the center of America, pretty close to the center of population, we have the worst living and housing conditions that I have seen anywhere in all the world. There is nothing in Calcutta, Johannesburg, or Hong Kong that equals the squalor of the East St. Louis slums. There are some miserable conditions around the world, but East St. Louis shows the greatest lack of organized capability to deal with the great challenges of democracy and crossbreeding world humanity. It is shocking.

Your educational forces, if competently organized and instrumented, should stimulate the self clean-up. The politicians won't clean up; the only hope is through education. This would be much better than building some kind of a socialized system where money is put up for more "buildings" just to keep the construction industry going and to provide jobs for political pay-offs. I am very glad that what I hope will be a powerful new magnitude of the educational system is coming to East St. Louis. This is appropriate. This is "Southern Illinois University's" historical opportunity.

I think that all the patterns I have been giving you are going to unfold rapidly and that primarily the individual is going to *study* at home. That is in the elementary, high school, and college years. Not until the graduate-work days begin will the individual take residence on campus. I am quite sure that the students of all ages will keep on going to "schoolhouses" to get *social experiences*—or to be "baby-sat." We will probably keep the schools open in the evening because of the growing need for baby-sitters. Real education, however, will be something to which individuals will discipline themselves spontaneously under the stimulus of their own ticker-tapes—their individually unique chromosomes. All people have their own chromosomal patterns. No two persons have the same appetite at the same time. There is no reason why they should. There is no reason why everyone should be interested in the geography of Venezuela on the same day and hour unless there is some "news" event there, such as a revolution. However, most of us are going to be interested in the geography of Venezuela at some time—our own time—but not all on the same day. *Simultaneous curricula are obsolete.* We must make all the information immediately available over the two-way TVs ready for the different individual human chromosomal ticker-tapes to call for it.

There are two more things I would like to talk about if we have the time. I am a comprehensive designer—that is, I try to organize all the data and challenges and problems in such a manner that they may be solved by inanimate technology, as I mentioned to you earlier, rather than by organization reforms. Therefore, when I talk about educational problems, I am interested in how these can be satisfied by some kind of physical apparatus along the lines of the trend requirements I have been outlining to you. The kind of equipment that would be involved would be such as the two-way TV and the Geoscope and also what I call *automated education facilities*. We know about teaching machines, etc., today, and much of this is sound. In our consideration of equipment we must also include the environment-controlling structures which will house the computer-integrated equipment and activities.

I am going to give you one more "big" introductory concept that may shed considerable light on these problems and may lead to acquisition of logical apparatus of solution. C. P. Snow, the writer, has a great following today. He writes about "two worlds." His two worlds are the literary world and the scientific world. In the literary world, man writes the books that people can understand with least effort. They seem to be good romance books because they seem to fit many lives. Science writes in ways that require complete dedication of effort to comprehend. Snow says the dichotomy between the two worlds began approximately two centuries ago with the inception of the industrial revolution. In England it is as yet evident that the popular writers of a century ago and since were not helped by the scientist. The scientist tended to be preoccupied, obscure, and not interested in the literary person's needs. A pertinent fact that Snow does not mention is that the important scientific events were often withheld from the public because of their unique military advantages. The scientist's information began to be the grist of the industrial technology. Scientists were intimately tied up with industry, even though they didn't look upon their personal work in terms of economics. Scientists were aloof to the ultimate fact that industry was the user of the information that they were able to gather.

The literary person, not understanding either science or its technology, developed an animosity toward industrialization. Snow points out for us that in America this dichotomy was in evidence, for instance, in Emerson and Thoreau, who were antipathetic to industrialization. As I grew up at the turn of the century I saw that society looked on industrialization as something noisy, smoky, and full of so-called artificialities. (In my viewpoint, there is no meaning to the word *artificial*. People can only do what nature permits them to do. They do not invent anything. They make discoveries of principles operative in nature and often find ways of generalizing those principles and reapplying them in surprise directions. That is called invention. But they do not do anything artificial. Nature has to permit it, and if nature permits it, it is natural. There is naught which is unnatural.)

The literary and popular concept of industrialization grew out of erroneous definitions and terms. The static viewpoint was seemingly supported by the Newtonian statement that "a body persists in a *state of rest* (or in a line of motion) except as affected by other bodies." Primarily the norm was "at rest," and changes were therefore abnormal and undesirable. Changes were exploited from time to time only because of military advantage or because people could make large amounts of money out of the changes and not because of any social voting that the changes were constructively desirable. The literati just didn't try to understand change, and they stayed apart from science and abhorred the changes. Snow says the gulf between the scientist and the literati is now so great that the chasm is no longer spannable. He feels there has now developed an irreparable dichotomy between the literary and scientific worlds. I do not agree with him as you shall learn.

Alfred North Whitehead came to Harvard University early in this twentieth century from the great universities of England. He said that one of the things that was very noticeable at Harvard was that this great private school was initiating a new kind of pattern. It was beginning to build and staff the great graduate schools. The graduate schools dealt in specializations. In England the special preoccupations could be taken up within the general university.

There were no special schools. Whitehead said that the American *populus* applauded the high specialization, and Whitehead saw that this pattern was being followed by the other leading private schools, colleges, and universities. Of course, the public schools and public universities immediately followed suit, taking on the graduate school patterns, because the political representatives of the public saw that their constituents would want the state school to incorporate these educational advances of the rich people's private schools. So specialization in graduate schools also became the "thing."

Whitehead said this meant that we deliberately sorted out the students, sieved them, picked out the bright ones, and persuaded the brights to stay in the university and to go on to the graduate school. This meant that we began to make specialists out of our bright ones. The bright ones within their own special category of their special school went on to develop further special nuances within their special areas. This all worked toward expertism and hybridism in the educational pursuits. It meant that bright ones would learn much about their special subject. The public thought this to be desirable, because people like the idea of an "all-star" team. They thought that if we took groups of all-stars and put them together our commonwealth would surely prosper.

Whitehead said, "So far so good, and everybody is applauding." But he then said that the educational hybridism would mean that these people who were of high intellectual capabilities would have very high intellectual integrity. As people of high intellectual integrity they would quickly discover that they were making great progress in highly specialized areas of inquiry and thus also they would know how little any other person outside of their own field could possibly understand of what was going on inside their own and inside any one field other than their respective specializations. Therefore, no specialist of integrity would think of going into some other expert's field and making quick assumptions as to the significance of that unfamiliar work. This would be considered preposterous. There would thus develop an increasing tendency to break down generalized communications and comprehensive prospecting between these experts. Certainly, they would not tend to join together and say: "I see I am developing this and you are developing that; if we associated them thus and so, such and such would be the economic consequences; therefore, let us do so by employing our credit as scientists with the banks in order to fund our undertakings." These people, Whitehead said, would do just the opposite and would become more and more subjective, growing into purer and purer scientists, to whom no banker would think of lending money on the basis of intellectual integrity alone. The scientists went in just the opposite direction of applied science. The more expert they were the less they would think of searching into the concept of how society might enjoy the fruits of their discoveries.

Whitehead pointed out that this system tended to break down the communication between the people of high intellectual capability in all special fields. Inasmuch as society wanted exploitation of the gains of their "all-star" teams, it meant that someone other than the prime intellects had to integrate and exploit their capabilities and their findings. Then Whitehead said—which came as quite a surprise—inasmuch as we have deliberately sorted out the bright ones from the dull ones, we have inadvertently created a class of dull ones. Just as in mining, we have a big pile of tailings, and no one thinks much about tailings because they are interested only in the high-grade, quick-cash ore and the net metal that is taken out of the latter. He said that inasmuch as the "bright ones" are not going to be able to realize, integrate, and exploit their own potentials we will have to leave it to the not-so-brights to put things together. This is what I have termed "Whitehead's dilemma."

I have developed "Whitehead's dilemma" a little further than he could go at that time. I find that there is a second grade of people who get passing marks, but are not selected to be specialists, who, however, though not "gleaming bright" have a dull polish and are good healthy folks who are liked by everybody. These second-grade "clean ones" become the first choice for executives in business, which does integrate potentials of demand and supply. Then as corporation executives these not-quite-so-brights take on the pure scientist experts and cultivate them like special hybrid egg-laying hens in special houses. The corporations take on the task of putting appropriate specializations together to exploit the synergetic advantages thus accruing. The business executives become the integrators of the bright ones' capabilities. Business executives themselves, however, tend to be specialists of a less fine order. Pretty soon, they will say, for instance: "We are in the automobile business and don't know anything about stockings; so we are just going to stick to our automobiles." They might also say: "We find that an automobile won't run across an open field. Therefore, it is only half of the invention-automotive transportation. The *highway* itself is a large part of the invention—high-speed highway transportation." Automobiling is schematically like a monkey wrench—the ratchet half is the "highway," and the thumb-screw-adjustable traveling jaw is the "automobile." The automobile is literally geared by its tire-treads to the road. So the business executives might say: "An automobile company could not possibly afford to build the highways—it is a very difficult political matter; you have to have costly condemnation proceedings and so forth to get a highway through; it is all so expensive that our company would never make a profit if we took the responsibility of providing highways. All we can produce is automobiles. To get the show going, however, we will have a little auto race track over here, and we will have automobile shows in many big cities and at county and state fairs. We will get people very excited about the way our automobile can go and how fascinating it looks." Thus it went, and the people began to envision personal use and enjoyment of the automobile "if only they had a highway." What the auto executive did was to excite the people into demanding highways for the cars.

We next come down to a duller class of not-so-brights—much duller—who didn't even go to college. This much duller class is that of the politicians. The politicians saw that the people in general wanted automobiles and wanted to "joy ride"; so they immediately voted for highways to get the peoples' votes for themselves.

Thus, a much bigger geographical pattern of the automobile emerged than the domain of the factory and the auto executive's specialized territory. The bigger pattern was the total highway system—state, interstate, and federal. We also find that generally speaking *the geographically larger the physical task to be done, the duller the conceptual brain that is brought to bear* upon the integration of the scientific discoveries and their technically realized applications. Finally, we get to international affairs, and you know what is happening today. The most highly polished of the dullest class, scientifically and intellectually speaking, may wear their striped pants very beautifully and be charming fellows, but they have not produced any mutually acceptable, constructive, world-peace-generating ideas. They traffic successfully only in peoples' troubles and emergency compromises. One of the great mistakes that society has been demonstrating in our last century has been that of leaving the most important problems to the men who are bankrupt in creative thinking ability. World War I marked the end of the old great masters of the water-ocean earth commerce. These were the world "bankers" who were the not-too-dull business executives who had high courage and coordination and who developed successful world-pattern cartels and trusts quite transcendentally to any one nation's antitrust laws or to any one nation's popular knowledge, advantaged by humanity's world-around preoccupations with their own respective domestic affairs. These old masters kept the world peoples in complete ignorance of their world planning and let it be thought that the latter was the consequence of their appointed local politicians' deliberations.

At Harvard just before World War I—and this was the time when I was having my little troubles there—the dilemma Whitehead was talking about was developing in a very interesting way. What Whitehead didn't ask was how Harvard could afford those graduate schools. The fact is that neither Harvard nor any other university has ever operated at a profit. Certainly, schools, colleges, and universities don't have surplus earnings accruing which they can reinvest. Establishing graduate schools wasn't something private colleges could do on their own. The explanation is that the graduate schools were *given* to Harvard and the other leading private universities.

The next interesting question is, *who gave* them the graduate *specialty* schools? Well, the people who gave Harvard the schools were primarily the partners of J. P. Morgan and Company or they were men who were founders or presidents of companies whose boards were run by J. P. Morgan. J. P. Morgan or his partners were at that time on the boards of nearly every important, powerful company in America. Morgan or his associates were also partners in the great unseen syndicate of world commerce mastery up to World War I.

If you were an invisible world master of the water-ocean earth you had to maintain the capability to create and run the top world navies—you had to have *physical control* of the biggest patterns. No matter what else we may say of these men today, they were magnificently imaginative big-scale operators. They had taken all that science had learned about energy and put it into their navies, faster, further, more accurately hitting power in order to keep in supreme command of physical affairs of humanity. Now, if you were world master, you would not be at all worried about being displaced by a *dull* one. You would only be apprehensive of and on guard against the bright ones. There is the old strategy of "divide and conquer." Anticipatory "divide and conquer" is more powerful than tardy "divide and conquer." The old masters, then, in order to prevent themselves from being displaced from their great ocean mastery deliberately went to work taking the young, bright ones as they came along, and divided them up anticipatorily into non-self-integratable *specializations,* which made them completely innocuous as challengers to comprehensive grand-strategy thinking and practical-affairs integration. The bright ones thus became subject to integration of their high potential only at the masters' command. That was the key to the world-pattern mastery up to World War I, when general literacy of the rising world democracies posed threats to the old masters' all but impregnable sinecure.

World War I marked the end of the old masters. The old masters had set up local rulers of their own choosing all around the world in the various nations. They invented the political nations. They invented the geographical names—Greece, Italy—their nations were welded out of many tribes and battles. The masters said to their head-men stooges: "You command and hold the port here. You are the strong man locally, and I will make you head man. You can stay head man because I have the line of supply of maximum hitting power and maximum energy duration. If anybody challenges you, you get the supplies and he doesn't, for I control the oceans which carry the supplies. Therefore, you are going to be able to win." This was the old and great pattern of world mastery. The local politician was a man (a king, or whatever) put into a position of strength by the great masters who themselves remained scrupulously invisible. They preferred to remain invisible. The more invisible they were the longer they could stay master. No challenges would arise, because there was nothing visible to challenge. Secrecy was one of the greatest of the tools of the old masters. The visible head man on the beach—the local head man—was strong, however, simply by virtue of the old invisible master.

The old masters went out with World War when their total gold resource became inadequate to accounting and accrediting of the extraordinary new magnitudes of wealth generated by industrialization. For instance, just in the United States alone, during World War I we produced $ 178 billion worth of "hard" or capital goods, compared with only $40 billion worth of gold extant in all the world to "pay for it." The gold was suddenly utterly inadequate to the new magnitudes of economic traffic. The masters had up to then run the world traffic with gold.

During World War I the incumbent world masters had been challenged by the organized "outs" who were the competitor commerce group of potential masters who were beginning to put the new potentials of science together faster than the old masters had seen fit to do. The "outs" invented going under the sea to break down the line of supply with submarines and going above the earth and sea with the airplane.

The old masters were being so vigorously challenged by the expansion of war patterns into new dimensions that they were about to be displaced, when suddenly a powerful scientific suggestion was made in England to the high command. A scientist said that there were ways in which the guns that reached the front could be made to last twice as long. He said: "Wouldn't this be as good as getting twice as many guns to the front? That is, even if the line of supplies were being critically slowed down by sinkings, the guns which did reach the front would last twice as long." The old high command said: "This is nonsense, but what do you have in mind?" Then the scientist said: "Well, we have had it here in the drawer since 1854; chrome nickel steel alloy." The old masters had never trusted anything they could not see, touch, or smell. They coordinated by virtue of their extraordinary sensorial ability—they were very *physical* human beings. They could count masts of ships swiftly, they could knock another guy down, they could play beautiful polo, and they could sail a very fast yacht. They did things in that sensorial way. But they were suspicious of anything invisible; internal structural functions of alloys were invisible; ergo, they were unaccredited by the old masters.

At the turn of the century we were coming to the point where there were the X-rays, alloys, and all kinds of invisible events of scientific specializations' discoveries, but the old masters didn't want any of that invisible phenomena let loose. They were suspicious of its portent. They said: "The kind of steel we are making is good—it is all right and will do." In America they owned U.S. Steel and so forth and were turning out what was called "mild steel." That is not a *specification* steel at all. It was the steel of the great rust dumps of pre-World War I. Finally, because of the submarine sinkings of their ships, in order to survive, the old masters had to unleash the manufacture of the alloys which made the tools last longer.

Thus in World War I, industry suddenly went from the visible to the invisible base, from the track to the trackless, from the wire to the wireless, from visible structuring to invisible structuring in alloys. The big thing about World War I is that people *went off the sensorial spectrum forever* as the prime criterion of accrediting initiations.

All major advances since World War I have been in the *infra-* and the *ultrasensorial* frequencies of the electromagnetic spectrum. All the important technical affairs of humanity today are invisible. This is the prime reason that the educational processes are now essential to survival, for only through highly literate disciplining may people control the invisible events of nature.

We see then that the old masters, who were sensorialists, had unleashed a Pandora's box of nonsensorially controllable phenomena, which they had avoided accrediting up to that time. At that great critical moment when they unleashed nonsensorially controllable physical phenomena they suddenly lost their true mastery, because from then on *they didn't personally understand what was going on*. If you don't understand you cannot master.

Since World War I, the old masters have been extinct. Because they operated always in secret, they of course didn't announce their own demise. As they died secretly they inadvertently left many accepted patterns, such as, for instance, the "head men" on the world thrones and the university patterns which Whitehead described. As the new problems brought about by the old

masters' demise arose, everybody began to turn to the local political head men and new head men who arose easily, pushing
over the old who no longer had the support of the now defunct
invisible masters.

After World War I in Germany—where the old masters had tak-
en all of the money away from their conquered challengers—the
people said: "There is a blast furnace right there; it already exists.
We know how to run it. There is the iron and there is the coal; why
don't we make steel?" They didn't have any money to put their
plans into effect; so they began using a new kind of wealth. They
said: "The only thing we need in order to use these resources is
the know-how which we have and the authority to do so." Since
all the money had been taken away by "reparations," the Germans simply forsook their old government who had agreed to the
reparations payments. They said: "We need a new political man,
and all we have to do is to get a couple of soldiers and some guns
and take over the post office. Then we take over the blast furnace
and we are in business." Thus it was discovered that you could
be in business without money, if you really had the scientific and
technical know-how.

That was also the pattern of new industrialism's initiations that
Russia copied from the United States, who had peacefully seized
or taken over as "government" in World War I all their prime pro-
ductive capabilities from the panicked old masters. Next, all the
dictatorships of Europe followed suit and seized their industries.
We went into a period of a new authority being vested in the political men who everybody locally had always thought of as all-
powerful. The transition of stooges into dictators of real power
was invisible and unreported. World people hadn't realized that
their local leaders' power sprang solely from the strength of the
invisible old masters secretly backing them. They thought of their
respective nations as sovereign and mystically endowed with unseen destiny of sovereign survival eminence. As a consequence,
since 1918 humanity, speaking always under their conditioned re-

flex concepts of static geographical "nations," has been challenging the local political heads with the responsibility of getting them out of their troubles. The suddenly, realistically "head men" haven't the slightest idea how to solve such problems. These were problems that only their old masters could solve. Nobody could have been duller in world stratagems than the political leaders of the world's many separate nations. Ruthless, tough bluffing became the new winning technique, but it was implemented by the politicians' exploitation of their respective hybrid, economic slaves, the scientific specialists.

In respect to "Whitehead's dilemma" everybody today tends to believe that specialization is the best way to earn a living, by establishing one's own special monopoly at some strategic point in the specialization network. As a consequence of comprehensively undertaken specialization we have today a general lack of comprehensive thinking. Specialists are therefore, in effect, slaves to the economic system in which they happen to function. The concept of inevitable specialization by the brightest has become approximately absolute in today's social-economic reflexing. The fixation is false and is soon to be altered.

I went to the U.S. Naval Academy at the moment in World War I when the grand masters and the British Navy for the first time in history had to acknowledge the American Navy as an equal and give it great support or *else* the old masters were probably going to lose their world mastery. As a consequence, the British Navy began to disclose to the U.S. Navy some of the inner secrets of its grand strategy. In addition to information given to top-rank admirals, much that was of basic strategic significance was disclosed to the young men who were being trained at the U.S. Naval Academy at that moment. To us at Annapolis there were disclosed some of the grand theories as well as special strategies used by the old masters. One of the prime theories I learned as one of those Naval Academy students was that in the *naval academies* of Britain, the

United States, and other European countries, in contradistinction to all private public universities and the military academies, they picked *bright ones* to be *trained* as *comprehensivists* rather than as *specialists.* In the armies, the officers became specialists for life as cavalrymen, artillerymen, etc., but the admirals were trained to function ultimately and exclusively as the *comprehensive* assistants to the great invisible masters who were running the earth.

This comprehensivity of admirals came about in the following manner. The old masters had commanded that the highest economic priority go toward using *everything* people had learned in physics and chemistry to produce the highest hitting-power navy, as the greatest tool with which to master the earth. This was due to the simple fact that you could carry bigger guns on ships than you could pull overland with horses. The Navy represented the focused objective for application of all that humanity knew about science, about mathematics, chemistry, and physics. All science was reduced to versatile, mobile practice in the Navy. Armies and fortresses were static and good for local war. Navies were the dynamic and the inherent world tools up to and through World War I.

In sending the Navy off to the high seas with all the nation's most important hardware, the nation had to develop admirals and captains whom the old masters could not only count on to be their most competent right-hand men but who could also be trusted with competent command and maintenance of this most powerful tool even when out of sight of the old masters. They had to have men who understood the world economic patterns as did the masters themselves. They needed admirals and officers in general who could take a great navy halfway around the world from home bases and build a new naval base, say in South America or in any other remote place, who understood technology in every way, who could handle thousands of men, millions of dollars, thousands of technical and psychological and economic problems—very *comprehensive* men, the antithesis of specialists. The training scheme in the Navy was to pick the brightest and send them first over to the Bureau of Ships where they could learn the theory and history of ships themselves and their great comprehensive patterning. Then the Navy Department deliberately rotated their officers' services, sending these men alternately to sea on different types of ships—every type and kind: submarines, battleships, destroyers, supply ships, and airships. Between ship assignments the Navy rotated its line officers into naval stations around the world. They rotated them back and forth, out of the ships into jurisprudence, into managing great naval shipyards which had the most powerful industrial tools of those days, and then to foreign embassies to get world statesmanship experience, and finally into the comprehensive world strategy studying at the Naval War College. The Navy's top-rank officers were always selecting the junior officers to be promoted. There was no automatic promotion by numbers in the advance ranks of the Navy, as there was in the Army. The admirals simply selected the two-and-one-half stripers who were most comprehensively capable and moved them up rapidly. The grand masters were then able to pick the officers they most trusted amongst those who had the most comprehensive ability.

After World War I the radio made physical centralization of political authority inevitable, and with political centralization and the demise of the old masters came the end of the autonomous admiral, ergo, the end of the need for comprehensive training. With this came oblivion for the concept of comprehensive capability and "finis" for the comprehensivist educational systems. Today the Navy, too, is specialized with "submarine officers" and "naval aviators," etc. By good fortune, I experienced the Naval Academy's last era of *comprehensive training*. I began in 1917 to study these great theories of Navy, the development of general logistical support of navies by great nations, and the establishment and maintenance of lines of supplies up to the critical moment of contact, when major naval engagements were decided on the first and second salvos, which demonstrated indubitably who had the best hardware, a condition that could only be altered by decades of new technology.

I saw that this comprehensivity of the top navy strategists all represented *great anticipatory design science, enormous vision, and supreme economic-wealth-investing-initiative.* I saw that the *theory* of Navy might be identified as a *comprehensive design problem.* The Navy and its industrial and logistic support of 1917 demonstrated well what I meant by *comprehensive anticipatory design science.* I saw that the matter of finally firing cannons from a moving ship on the heaving sea at another moving ship on the heaving sea represented all the variables that would be operative in firing from any steerable planet against any other steerable planet in the free heavens. All the mathematical complexities of all the variables of Universe were inherent in the problem. Therefore, I said this special Navy logistics and ballistics case might be generalized subjectively into what I call the *comprehensive minimum-maximum family of universally variable factors.* These could then be generalized objectively as *a comprehensive anticipatory design science* which could be applied to any special case such as world naval mastery or world industrialization planning, etc.

I considered it inadequate to apply this science only to the Navy, and I intuited that *comprehensive anticipatory design science* might be applied also to the larger question of *how we can make life on earth a general success for all people* instead of assuming negatively that success and even prolonged survival were for the rare and fortunate few. I felt strongly that there might be a day when society would need to state its objective in just that way. I found myself working toward comprehensive strategies and capabilities which brought me to the only truly generalized and, therefore, most powerful tool of all, and that was mathematics itself. Mathematics has been on highest priority in my grand strategy. The reason I spoke to you earlier about my having some kind of unique behavior pattern in my day is because I am a *comprehensivist* in contradistinction to a *specialist,* and nowadays there are approximately none other than specialists. I don't know anybody else who has actually been operating with the same comprehensive strategy as mine in my day, for my Navy friends were comprehensive specialists, whereas I became a comprehensive generalist.

At the World Affairs Conference in Colorado this last week, they brought Ludwig von Bertalanffy together with me on five panels. Ludwig von Bertalanffy is a great biologist. He is in the front ranks of the "academy." As a great scientist in biology, he discovered that there were comprehensive system behaviors in nature unpredicted by the behaviors of the systems' components, a phenomenon known to scientists as synergy. Von Bertalanffy, along with other mathematicians who had discovered synergy in the theories of games and so forth, began to discover that there were complex patterns which could never be apprehended, understood, operated on, or dealt with if we approached them only in terms of their separate elements; that is, *literally* in an *elementary* manner. Our whole educational process, all the way up from the elementary school, is one of taking children who have an innate comprehensive coordinate capability (not only to teach themselves to walk but to be interested in the *heavens*) and give them differentiated parts—elements to work with. The prime patrons of the planetariums and the like are the children, because they are spontaneously interested in the universe, that is, in the comprehensive rather than in the speciality—the elements. We get them to school, and we say forget the universe, and we give them A, B, and C. We go toward the very opposite of comprehensiveness. We go to the specialization right away. We render the children more and more specialized from elementary school onward. Ludwig von Bertalanffy began to find that nature, as biology, did not tend toward hybridism or more limited specialization by itself. Nature reverted toward generalism. Nature tended to work toward broader adaptation, ergo, more comprehensive capabilities. As a consequence, Dr. von Bertalanffy was the scientist who developed an expression you are quite familiar with today—General Systems Theory. Von Bertalanffy employs his General Systems Theory subjectively. He agreed with me that my *comprehensive anticipatory design science* is an objective employment of systems theory and that I had discovered the same phenomenon that he had discovered through completely different circumstances.

If we apply General Systems Theory to the analysis of our total world problem, today we obtain an excellent view of the techno-scientific, industrial theatre and the *socio-economic drama* in which our swiftly evolving educational processes are going to function and we can see far more clearly what the roles therein may be of the kinds of new educational developments which I have been describing to you. We will also be able to comprehend better the problems that were insurmountable to the old "world masters" and how the coming universities may now solve them under the newer circumstances.

Our pertinent *socio-economic drama* begins at the first moment in history when economic data was coming in from all around the earth to one place on earth—England. Thomas Malthus, integrating that data, discovered that the world's people were multiplying their numbers more rapidly than they were producing goods to supply themselves. Malthus's discovery coincided with the moment when Darwin was discovering his theory of evolution and adopting his hypothesis that evolution was predicated upon survival of the fittest. As a consequence, Malthus's pattern seemed to validate survival of the fittest among human beings as fulfilling Darwin's scientific law. Up to that moment in history, whether world societies fared well or ill had seemed to be a matter of fate or of a whimsical decision of the gods. Suddenly the Malthusian concept of survival-of-the-fittest, i.e., you-or-me, not both—"you have to make a choice"—seemingly became a stark scientific fact which confronted the political and economic leaders of nations. From that moment in history it was clearly a matter of "you or me," and the leaders of great nations felt it was their obviously mandated responsibility to be sure that it was not their own nations that went down. At this present 1961 moment in history the "you or me" motivation founded on Malthus still constitutes the mainspring of world political policy and action.

The solutions under the Malthusian "you or me" challenge fell into two main political categories: (1) ruthless but often polite decimation of the unsupportable fractions, or leaving the unsupportable fractions to their unhappy fate; (2) socialism—the theory of austerity for all and sharing of the inadequacy with slow mutual approach to certain untimely demise.

In view of the seemingly scientific inexorability of the Malthusian concept, it comes as a great surprise that in this century a new pattern has emerged which not only questions the fundamental validity of the Malthusian and Darwinian theories but even seems to promise their complete invalidation in both the economic and social domains.

At the turn of the century the technology of the industrial revolution was beginning to integrate, developing patterns of higher leverage in the doing of humanity's work than had been anticipated. As of 1900, less than 1 percent of humanity was participating in the high advantages of the industrial network. (I developed a physical measure of what I mean by participating in the industrial equation when I was Technical Consultant to *Fortune* magazine in 1933. When the equivalent of the physical foot-pounds per hour work that could be done by 200 human slaves was available and being used in electrical and other energy units in the industrial equation per each human family of five members, I rated this family as an industrial "have" family.) The intertechnology jelling was occurring at such an important rate at the turn of the century that by 1914 and the beginning of World War I, the percentage of human family participation in the industrial network advantage had grown from less than 1 percent to 6 percent. It was unquestionably this swift integration of new levels of technology that emboldened the political world "outs" to challenge the political "ins" in World War I. As World War II began, 20 percent of humanity was participating in the advantages of the industrial network. At the present moment approximately 43 percent of humanity is participating in the ever-higher advantages of the integrated industrial network.[11]

This emergence of a new economic pattern in which humanity's relative survival advantage is amplified is news to you. This is not surprising, however, because it is a discovery of my own and has not been widely published. The *New York Times* made mention of my discovery of this economic curve in 1952.[12] The curve of acceleration[13] of those participating in industrialization indicates that the whole of the human family will be participating in the highest technical advantages before the end of the twentieth century and at a level of human satisfaction as yet not even dreamed of by any person.

To understand the surprising significance of this curve it must be understood that what I speak of as the industrial network embraces *all the resources of the earth* that enter into the establishment and maintenance of the industrial processes. As the percentage of world population participating in the high industrial network advantage increased from 1 percent to 43 percent, it meant that the total of organized world tonnages in metallic and metabolic resources was exclusively supplying only 1 percent, then 6 percent, then 20 percent, then 43 percent of the world's population. During this first half of the twentieth century of realized industrialization, the world's population has been increasing at

11 In 2001, 56 percent (3.4 billion of 6.1 billion) were out of poverty, using current notions of "middle income" and "high income" families. Note: "middle income" on a global development basis means "incomes of a few thousand per year," which is not equivalent to measures of "middle income" in wealthy countries. Jeffrey Sachs, *The End of Poverty: Economic Possibilities for Our Time* (New York, 2005), chapter 1.

12 Walter Dorwin Teague, "Gains of Industry Predicted for All: Engineer Tells Design Meeting World Should be Completely Industrialized by Year 2000," *New York Times*, June 26, 1952.

13 Fuller published a chart presenting this analysis in 1952. See the introduction to this volume, note 2, p. 8; and R. Buckminster Fuller, *Ideas and Integrities: A Spontaneous Autobiographical Disclosure* (Baden, 2010), p. 333 (fig. 10).

a faster rate than additional resources have been discovered. *That is, the per capita ratio of world copper, mined or unmined, or of iron, mined or unmined, has been continually decreasing.* Therefore, these ratio increases in the industrially advantaged numbers-served have not been the result of the addition of more resources, but the consequence of the scientifically designed multiplication of the technical performance or relative efficiency of output per units of invested resource. Transferring communication from wire to wireless is a typical means of doing more with less. At present we are engaged in converting all of the two-ton American automobiles into twice as many one-ton higher performance automobiles.

I am confident that the architects and engineers of the world will not claim that they have been consciously engaged either singly or coordinately in the deliberate increasing and improving of the *overall world performance ratios* of the comprehensive world resources pattern. I am confident they will agree with me that this was not the declared policy of any nation or of any business corporation or of any professional groups or individuals. How then did it all come about? The answer is that the performance increase has been a by-product of the development of weaponry and of the concomitant tools-to-make-tools investments to produce and support that massive weaponry. The fabulous capital investments for the weaponry and its supporting effort were all predicated upon the Malthusian "you or me" concept. As each level of weaponry advance becomes progressively obsolete by a new level of attainment, the technology which arose to produce and support the previous top level then becomes available to world society for everyday technical-economical satisfactions.

The change in the world's standard of living, its utter change of humanity's ecological patterning from yesterday's little, local, on-foot, visible horizon sweepout, to the world-around sweepout of 1961 has been, then, an inadvertent expediency of secondary commerce sequitur to our preoccupation with weaponry.

Two and a half trillion dollars were invested by the nations of the earth in the subsidy of the airplane as a weapon in the first half-century of the airplane.[14] This amounts to sixty-two times the value of all the gold in the world. The two and one-half trillion was the cumulative value of a regenerative investing pattern employing the tooled wealth to create higher tooled capability and to inhibit more energy from world energy patterning by shunting previously unharnessed energy into humanity's industrial networks to apply it to the end of his ever-regeneratively larger and more incisive levers. The cumulative reinvestable capital-capability-wealth is vast and has made gold and the concept of intrinsic wealth utterly obsolete, for the harnessed industrial-energy and its tooled-up-capability and the reworked and recirculated physical chemistry and the *ever improving* know-how altogether integrate as the real wealth of the world.

How did it happen that the native preoccupations of men in weaponry continually improved the performance per units of invested resources? It was because the ability to carry the hitting power of the weaponry the greatest distance in the shortest time involved ships, and ships had limited displacement, due to nature's pattern of floatability. Therefore, the design challenge was to produce the most powerful ship with the least weight invested in the ship, thus enabling it to carry the greatest load of weaponry, ammunition, and fuel to get it there faster. As we went from the ships of the sea to the ships of the air, the performance per pound of the equipment and fuel became of even higher importance than on the sea. Finally, with the breakthrough to rocketry, we see a transition of startling magnitude in speed, distance, and energy load carried per weight of vehicle or ship and its fuel.

Architects know that neither they nor their patrons have ever been concerned with the weights of their buildings or with any

---

14 $ 2.5 trillion in 1960, adjusted for inflation using the Consumer Price Index (CPI), is $ 18.22 trillion in 2009 dollars. http://www.bls.gov/data/inflation_calculator.htm (accessed July 15, 2009).

ratings of performance per units of weight investment. Neither the architects nor society know what buildings weigh. Society knows well what the *Queen Mary* and the Douglas DC-8 weigh[15]; the public knows what the sea and air ships' performance capabilities are. The public thinks of performance-per-pound ratings, but the world of housing, the world of architecture, has always been a world of opinionated dealing with the left-overs after the high-priority technologies have been applied exclusively to the weaponry and its supporting industries.

It is a fundamental characteristic of industrial evolution that each successful invention is followed by a period of expansion of the use of the invented tools in which more performance by that type of tool is accomplished only by more of those tools of bigger and bigger capacity until the elephantine level is attained; e.g., in ocean ships, the *Queen Mary*. Thereafter there develops a period of converting the doing-more-with-*more* phase of that tool into a doing-more-with-*less* phase, which uses new alloys and techniques, accomplishing as much as the elephantine with a tool of lesser size; e.g., the *United States*, carrying the same number of passengers and tonnage of cargo at the same speed with 30 percent less tonnage and size than the *Queen Mary's*.

Then follows a third period in which an entirely new type of tool does the same task with a small fraction of the weight of the previously invested resources, but only with an investment of fabulous magnitudes of completely weightless scientific activity. For instance, one jet airplane succeeds in one year in out-performing the annual trans-Atlantic passenger ferrying capability of the *Queen Mary* or the *United States*, with of course many more accomplished round-trips of its diminutive passenger capacity. Previously complex radio tubes replaced by transistors are typical of the progressive diminution in size and weight of the newly invented tool for an old task.

15 The *Queen Mary* weighs 81,237 gross tons; a DC-8 weighs 355,000 pounds at takeoff when completely full.

When Sputnik went into the sky the now suddenly "elephantine" airplane weaponry system yielded its premiership to a weapon transportation system with enormously increased hitting power which is not only far swifter but which also employs a minuscule fraction of the physical resource tonnage in its supporting tools as well as in the weapons themselves. This new, vastly more efficient system requires, however, a fabulous, abstract (no weight) investment of the essential scientific resource, i.e., humanity's disciplined mind activity. With the obsolescence of the aircraft industry as a prime *weaponry* resource, 90 percent of that industry's now obsolete massive high-performance technology production capacity was potentially released for application to *livingry*.

The world's architects are faced with the fact that the munitions industry managements will be henceforth increasingly panicked to obtain economic survival tasks for their soon-to-be 90-percent-unused aircraft technology production capacity, and will attempt to apply that capacity to the great industrial vacuum, the building industry, using their own ignorant opinions to determine the designs of products to be produced and, as already demonstrated, will produce aluminum versions of Cotswold cottages and other technical substitutions for components of conventional building, such as curtain walls and partitioning, all of which are of the design conception level which serves only 40 percent of humanity with 100 percent of the world's resources.

Neither the philosophy nor the fundamental volition, transcendental to immediate economic survival considerations, exists in the aircraft munitions industry that might otherwise bring it to the inauguration of unprecedented world-around, air-deliverable, high-standard livingry systems designed at an entirely new level of design invention competence as is now feasible within the aircraft technology and production capacity. In the latter now exists the potential of evolving augmentation of technical performance in livingry adequate to supply and maintain the advanced service of 100 percent of humanity with less than

100 percent of the world's resources and is feasible through design ingenuity and only through design ingenuity applied directly to livingry.

We discover in the picture that I have given you the fact that the upping of the performance per pound of the world's resources for improving standards of living has never been a direct objective of the politicians or the military servants of the politicians. Gradually we realize the startling significance of this emerging pattern of improvement of the performance of the world's resources as applied secondarily to "livingry" of humanity. This unheralded, unpremeditated emergent pattern indicates the inexorable realization of 100-percent industrialization of humanity, to be realized before 2000 A.D. but only as a by-product of humanity's negative lethal warfare preoccupation, which means that it will be realized only through an increasing succession of world-around military-threat emergencies of the kind which humanity now finds itself apparently helplessly enmeshed in.

Because the forward transformation of the resources from their going-low efficiency functions into other functions of higher performance represents a continual revolution in design, it is a pattern that could be mastered by people as *comprehensive anticipatory design scientists*. There are at present no design scientists. Architects and engineers are the nearest approach to such a profession. If, however, architects and engineers, as has been their custom, wait for a patron to command their services before they engage in their designing practice, it is easy to see that neither the politician nor the great industrialist nor any private patron will engage the architectural profession in this anticipatory design command of the total world-resources investment and total world technical evolution, because the politico and the industrialist and the private patron are all still convinced of the inexorableness of the Malthusian "you or me" and the "survival only of the fittest."

What I now propose is that all the universities around the world be encouraged to invest the next ten years in a continuing problem of *how to make the total world's resources, which now serve only 43 percent,*[16] *serve 100 percent of humanity through competent complex design science.*

The general theory of education at present starts students off with elementary components and gradually increases the size of the complex of components with which the student will be concerned. The scheme is to go from the particular toward the whole but never to reach the whole. In many of the architectural schools first-year students are given a problem in terms of a country town and have to plan and design the buildings for that country town. The next year they must do a larger town, a small industrial town. In the third year they are engaged in a large industrial city, and in their fourth year they are engaged with the largest cities, such as London or New York. The schools never reach out to national, let alone world, problems. As a consequence, local town planning everywhere is almost completely invalidated by the sweep of world events. The automobile highway clover-leaf programs are completely inadequate to the concept of total humanity being advantaged with their own vehicles. Parking problems continually frustrate and negate the too local, too small horizon of town planning.

The first year's total world planning by the students and its designed implementation may be expected to disclose great amateurishness and inadequacies, but out of the criticisms of the amateurishness and the inadequacies should emerge criticisms from the politicos, from the great economists, and the great industrialists, excited by the students' plans treading on their doorsteps, out of which criticism the next year's round of world designing by the students may be greatly advantaged. The second, third, and fourth years should show swift acceleration in the comprehension of the

16 See note 11, p. 94.

problem and the degree of satisfaction of the problem. If the students present their progressive yearly solutions in documentary moving pictures they may be distributed around the world and may be called up over two-way TV.

The world planning by the students must be predicated upon the concept of first things first, upon a scheduled hierarchy of events. These have been variously known as five-year plans, seven-year plans, etc., by the nations of the earth who have gone swiftly from almost complete "have noneness" and illiteracy to powerful "haveness" and almost 100-percent literacy. As each unindustrialized nation undertakes industrialization, the rate at which it accomplishes each of the progressive plan stages contracts—that is, the curve of overall world industrialization—is constantly accelerating.

At the present moment in history, what is spoken of as world policy by the respective nations consists essentially of their own special plans to bring about conditions which would uniquely foster their respective kinds of survival in the Malthusian "you or me-ness." For any one of the world policies of any of the nations or groups of nations to become a world plan would mean that approximately one-half of the world's nations would have to surrender their sovereignty and would mean the development of a highly biased plan as applied to the whole. In the nature of political compromises it is logical to assume that the world policy of any one political nation will never succeed in satisfying comprehensive world planning.

It is clearly manifest that students and scientists are able to think regarding such world planning in a manner utterly transcendental to any political bias. My experience around the world and amongst the students tells me that the students themselves tend always to transcend political bias and that *all of them are concerned with the concept of making the world work through competent design.* In much investigation and inquiry I have had no negative response to the program of organization of the student capability to the upping of the performance of the world resources to serve 100 percent of humanity by peaceful, comprehensive laboratory experiment and progressive design revolution.

At the present time, in this era of exaggerated specialization, the special knowledge and capabilities thus developed are rapidly drained off from the university into large corporations and into government defense bureaucracies or military bureaucracies. The scientists and inventors are wary under these circumstances, and it is probable that if the students who are potential comprehensive anticipatory design scientists are progressively and adequately disciplined to breadth of capability in chemistry, physics, mathematics, bio-chemistry, psychology, economics, and industrial technology they will swiftly and ably penetrate the most advanced recesses of the scientific minds resident in the university, and as their programs evolute from year to year in improving capability the students will be able to bring the highest integral scientific resources of humanity to bear upon their solutions of dynamic world town planning and its design instrumentation and operational regeneration.

The comprehensive world resources data now exist in a number of establishments, but are primarily available to all the universities of the world through UNESCO. What UNESCO does not have, it is in a good position to direct the researcher to acquire successfully. Our Geoscope would be dramatic aid in such resource-use planning and its communication to world news distributing services.

I have discussed this potential development of a comprehensive world strategy by the students who are potential comprehensive anticipatory design scientists with faculties and students on both sides of the world political curtains and have had unanimously enthusiastic reactions. The project has the extraordinary virtue that it inherently avoids political bias; therefore, there will be no suggestion of any subversive activity by any participants. It may receive political support from all sides by virtue of the important knowledge that will accrue. I am confident that there are many other human beings who at this moment envision analogous developments, all of which are symptomatic of a maturely emergent world trending whose exact modes of realization are unpredictable. But we may assume that the great, looming, humanity-favoring events of tomorrow will occur as the result of our adoption of comprehensive anticipatory design science within the universities.

I told your architect, Mr. Obata, the other day that I think you can break down your comprehensive educational undertaking into two main categories: one, all the *subjective disciplines,* and two, all the *objective disciplines.* (Phrases like the College of Fine Arts really have no meaning any more.) These would be objective disciplines in contradistinction to the subjective "pure" science data-gathering disciplines. It is very appropriate to have all kinds of subjective disciplines where people learn how to gather data faithfully and how to analyze their data, but they don't have to comprehend the data; they are not asked to comprehend. There is often not enough pattern to warrant having suspicion or intuition as to the significance of the considered pattern —or *lack* of describable pattern. Those are the subjective disciplines. It is only after the subjective that we get the objective.

I think that one of the most important events of the educational revolution is the present realization that we are going to discover that children are born comprehensively competent and coordinate and that they are capable of treating with large quantities of data and families of variables right from the start.

When parents make babies they don't know what they are making. They don't know how to make what they make. All they do is "press a button." Our and our babies' brains have a quadrillion times a quadrillion atoms already operative in coordinate patterning operation utterly transcendental to our conscious control. A quadrillion times a quadrillion atoms operative subconsciously in most extraordinary coordination make it possible, for example, for me to be communicating with you. We don't have anything consciously to do with the fundamentals of our communicating capability. Nor do we have anything to do consciously with pushing a million hairs out of our heads at preferred rates, colors, and shapes. We don't know how to consciously coordinate our heart beating and our breathing. We don't know at all how we charge energies back into the various glands of our systems. We really don't know what is going on at all, but we do coordinate it all subconsciously. What we do have in the brain is an extraordinary, orderly pattern manipulating capability to deal with that quadrillion times a quadrillion invisible atoms. This is all born into the child. The parent doesn't consciously put it there. People may take no credit for the fundamentals of their relative success upon earth.

I will say that it is very clear to me that when children stand up, breathing and coordinating all these complex patterns by themselves and get their own balance and start drinking in the patterns of cosmos and earth they are apparently spontaneously interested in coordinating the total information—the total stimulation. They crave to understand—to comprehend. That is why they ask their myriad questions.

I am quite confident we are going to find ways of helping children to coordinate their spontaneous comprehension of the *whole* instead of becoming specialists without losing any of the advantages gained by yesterday's exclusive specialization. With general comprehension there will also come an entirely new way of looking at our mutual problems around the earth. We will not be easily influenced by ignorant persuasion and propaganda, such as pronouncements that "we are against this person and that person," and so forth. We are going to look at our problems quite differently than we do now. There will be a coordinated comprehensive continuation of development of the child in appreciation of the subconsciously coordinate design of humans not forcing them into prolonged special focus, yet accomplishing with automated tools and instruments far greater probing than was accomplished by the utter specialist while conserving the comprehensive comprehension of the significance to society of the increasing flow of discovered data.

Next, let us think carefully and daringly of the equipment we will need and that we won't need for the large, new research establishments for students staying longer and longer at the university, as the new major industry of mankind. At M.I.T., for instance, where I visited as lecturer for eight years, there are rooms full of special and expensive apparatus which everyone thought would put M.I.T. at the top of the heap. Room after room of this equipment is now obsolete—at best these collections of machinery make a dull museum.

The first time I met Harold Cohen, now Director of Southern Illinois University's Design Research Department, was at the Institute of Design in Chicago. Chermayeff, its head, had his carpenter spend practically all his summer making drawing boards for my room, assuming without asking that I would need them. I did not. Harold will remember that the first thing we did in that room was to put the drawing boards up along the wall to use them only as shelves. Why were those drawing boards obsolete? In the world of designing today, such as in the great aircraft companies, you don't make drawings as in the past, which drawings are handed over to a carpenter, who in turn scales them off and makes from them a physical reality device or structure. Today we make only *schematics* and *schedules* of *data,* because the tolerances involved are subvisible—nobody could "lay it out." The machines have to index it. You don't need a detailed drawing; we do not make that kind of communication to a craftsman anymore; but all the schools go on teaching that we do. The data no longer goes to the craftsman; it goes to the tools. The idea of drafting measured details is going to become obsolete. We don't want any more measured detail drafting. What we want are the people who get the fundamental concept, the information significance and can do some comprehensive thinking regarding that information. They will put the data into the information machines, and it will be processed by automation into physical realization of their effective thinking. We don't need many of the myriad of "things" we have had in schools.

I would counsel you in your deliberation regarding getting campuses ready now to get general comprehensive environment controls that are suitable to all-purposes like a circus. A circus is a transformable environment. You get an enclosure against "weather" that you can put up in a hurry, within which you can put up all kinds of apparatus—high trapezes, platforms, rings, nets, etc. You can knock it down in a few minutes. That is the way the modern laboratory goes. In laboratories you can get the generalized pipette or whatever it is, the crucible, and the furnace. You can put the right things together very fast, rig them up, get through the experiment, knock it down. It's one clean space again. You want clean spaces. The circus concept is very important for you. I would get buildings where it is possible for many to meet. On the Carbondale campus you have succeeded in getting some good auditoriums—but we need more auditoriums and more auditoriums time and time again. We want places where there is just a beautiful blank floor and beautiful blank walls upon which to cast our pictures or apply crayons. You don't have to put any "architecture" there at all. You don't have to build any sculptured architecture—use the ephemeral. Work from the visible to the invisible very rapidly.

I would not waste dollars on great, heavy, stone masonry and any kind of Georgian architecture, and I would forget all the old architecture and even the curricula patterns of any schools before this moment. You might better consider putting up one big one-half-mile-diameter geodesic dome over your whole campus and thereafter subdivide off local areas temporarily for various activities.

Anything that is static, forget it. Work entirely toward the dynamic. Get yourself the tools and ways of enclosing enormous amounts of space, and make it possible for large numbers of human beings to come together under more preferred conditions than have ever before come together. Then give them large clear spaces so that their privacy results from having sufficient distance between people or groups of people. Get over the ideas of partitions. Partitions are like socialism. They came out of living and working in fortresses where there wasn't enough room to go around, so they put up partitions—really making cells. Partitions simply say you shall not pass. That's all they do. They are improvised to make that which is fundamentally inadequate work "after a fashion."

There are four kinds of privacy: if I can't touch you, we're *tactilely* private; if I can't smell you, we are *olfactorily* private; if I can't hear you, we're *aurally* private; and if I can't see you, we are *visually* private. Just a little space will take care of the first three. For the fourth—since we can see a great distance—all we need are delicate occulting membranes, possibly rose bushes or soap bubbles or smoke screens.

These are the devices you will have to get to handle emergency after emergency of swift transformations. You should get plenty of good real estate, which you, President Morris, have a proclivity for. I continually admire your intuitions in getting the countryside organized so that it can be of service to vast numbers of people without ruining that countryside.

As examples of the kind of environment controlling facility to which I have been referring, think of the fifty-five-foot-diameter Marine Corps geodesic domes. We began flying them around by helicopter in 1954. Last year we sold to the Ford Motor Company, from my office in Raleigh, North Carolina, two domes, not 55-footers but 114-footers. That is, each had 10,000 square feet of floor space. Each was an auditorium with a dark skin. One helicopter picked each one up. Ford started one of the domes in Alabama and one in Texas and moved them north. They didn't fly them most of the time; they disassembled and reassembled them, but they discovered they could fly them. One helicopter could pick up 10,000 square feet of floor space—that's quite a lot—and move it from place to place at a mile a minute. Considering the rate at which the helicopters are now increasing the loads they can carry and the rate at which I'm finding I can make lighter and lighter buildings, I can tell you that within five years I will be able to fly the clear-span cover for a baseball stadium (14½ acres) fully assembled, delivering it to its site at sixty knots. This is what is coming. Get yourselves the right geographical bases; you're very smart in getting your airplanes. Get lots of real estate and lots of airplanes and helicopters—get mobility. Get the most comprehensive generalized computer setup with network connections to process the documentaries that your faculty and graduate-student teams will manufacture objectively from the subjective gleanings of your vast new world- and Universe-ranging student probers. Get ready the greatest new educational facility at the approximate dynamic population center of the North American continent, assuming that any dreamable vision of technical advance will be a reality and that humanity is about to demonstrate competence beyond our estimates of yesterday and today. "Shoot for the moon"—yesterday a statement of lunacy—only a lunatic would now deny that this is the most evidently "next" practical objective of humanity.

Emergent Humanity
Its Environment and Education

An educational revolution is upon us.

One of the most important events of this peaceful but profound revolution is our dawning discovery that the child is born comprehensively competent and coordinate, capable of treating with large quantities of data and families of variables right from the start.

Every well-born child is originally geniused, but is swiftly de-geniused by unwitting humans and/or physically unfavorable environmental factors. "Bright" children are those less traumatized. Of course, some children have special inbred aptitudes and others, more crossbred, are more comprehensively coordinated.

But the new life is inherently comprehensive in its apprehending, comprehending and coordinating capabilities. The child is interested in Universe, and asks universal questions.

This propensity of the child toward comprehensivity, given a properly patterned environment, is attested in such works as Benjamin Bloom's *Stability and Change in Human Characteristics,*[1] and Wilder Penfield and Lamar Roberts's *Speech and Brain Mechanisms.* [2]

1   Benjamin S. Bloom, *Stability and Change in Human Characteristics* (New York: Wiley, 1964).

2   Wilder Penfield and Lamar Roberts, *Speech and Brain Mechanisms* (Princeton: Princeton University Press, 1959). See also Wilder Penfield, "The Uncommitted Cortex," *Atlantic Monthly,* July 1964.

1968. This essay was first published as the prologue for George L. Stevens and R. C. Orem, *The Case for Early Reading* (St. Louis, 1968).

Through electro-probing of the human brain, we are beginning to understand something of its energy patterns and information processing. We apparently start life with a given total-brain-cell capacity, component areas of which are progressively employed in a series of events initiated in the individual's brain by chromosomic "alarm clocks." Put your finger in the palm of a newborn baby's hand and the baby will close its tiny hand deftly around your finger, for its tactile apprehending organism is operative in superb coordination. Soon the "alarm clock" calls the hearing function into operation, and on its own unique schedule the baby will also see.

In a stimulating environment, the brain's chromosomic alarm clocks and "ticker tape" instructions inaugurate use of the child's vast inventory of intercoordinate capabilities and faculties. Children are not in fact taught and cannot be taught by others to inaugurate these capabilities. They teach themselves—if given the chance—at the right time. This provision of environmental experience conducive to the child's intellectual development has been termed the "problem of the match" by J. McV. Hunt, in his *Intelligence and Experience,* [3] he also speaks of "motivation inherent in information processing."

Bloom finds that environment has its greatest influence on a human characteristic—such as intelligence—during the period of time in which the characteristic is undergoing its greatest rate of growth or change. Thus, by age four, 50 percent of the child's total capacity to develop its I.Q. is realized.

If not properly attended to and given the chance to function, despite the brain's alarm-clock inauguration of progressive potentialities in the first four years, the brain mechanisms can be frustrated and can shut off the valves of specific capacities and capabilities to learn, then or later on, in the specific areas. The

3 J. McV. Hunt, *Intelligence and Experience* (New York: Ronald, 1961). See also his "Motivation Inherent in Information Processing and Action," in *Motivation and Social Interaction,* ed. J. D. Harvey (New York: Ronald).

capabilities need not necessarily be employed to an important degree immediately after being triggered into inception, but must upon inception be put in use and kept in use as active tools in the human coordinating capability, else they will squelch themselves, "shut themselves off," not necessarily irreparably, but usually so.

Piaget has said: "The more children have seen and heard, the more they want to see and hear." I add: "The more children have coordinated, the more they want to coordinate."

By age eight, 80 percent of the child's total capability to self-improve I.Q. in learning how to learn is activated. By age thirteen, 92 percent of this capability is self-started into usability and by seventeen, the final 8 percent of the total capacity to coordinate and apprehend, to comprehend and teleologically employ input data, has become operative.

Traditionally, the great bulk of government educational funds has been applied after the critical birth-to-eight period during which 80 percent of the child's educational capacity is being established. In the light of recent research findings, our input of personnel, funds, and energy into education must be reversed.[4] A powerful case can be made for inverting the educational structure—for paying parents or other people responsible for the most important, formative years more than college professors—in due ratio to their greater responsibility. O. K. Moore, of "talking typewriter" fame, has made a similar suggestion.[5]

Let us focus our efforts to help the new life on the critical first thirteen years, when approximately 92 percent of brain function is progressively and automatically "turned-on," "tuned-in,"

4   Operation Head Start, Title I of ESEA and recent related programs appear to represent a more realistic utilization of resources. See "The Big Federal Move Into Education," *Time,* April 30, 1965.

5   O. K. Moore, *Autotelic Responsive Environments and Exceptional Children* (Hamden, Conn.: Responsive Environments, Inc., 1963). See also Maya Pines, "How Three-year-olds Teach Themselves to Read—and Love It," *Harper's,* May 1963, p. 61.

"tuned-out," or "shut-off," in direct response to the positives or negatives of the individual's environmental experiences and potentials, keeping in mind that by age four 50 percent of brain function is realized, which must be properly set in use and kept in use.

Not only intelligence is developed during these formative years, but also the basic characteristics determining much of the individual's personality and behavior as well.

Will the older, adult life demonstrate that it really wants more life by designing an environment to foster the new child-life adequately—to nourish the unfolding flowers of the "cortical gardens?" As I predicted in the *Saturday Review:*

> In the next decade, society is going to be preoccupied with the child because through the behavioral sciences and electrical exploration of the brain we find that, given the right environment and thoughtful answers to his questions, *children have everything they need educationally right from birth.* We have thought erroneously of education as the mature wisdom and over-brimming knowledge of the grownups injected by the discipline pump into the otherwise "empty" child's head. Sometimes, parents say "don't" because they want to protect the child from getting into trouble. At other times when they fail to say "no" the child gets into trouble. The child, frustrated, stops exploring. It is possible to design environments within which the child will be neither frustrated nor hurt, yet free to develop spontaneously and fully without trespassing on others. I have learned to undertake reform of the environment and not to try to reform humanity. If *we design the environment properly,* it will permit children and adults to develop safely and to behave logically. [6]

6   R. Buckminster Fuller, "What I Have Learned: How Little I Know," *Saturday Review,* November 12, 1966, p. 70.

The work of Bloom, Erikson, [7] and others reveals that this environment must promote *trust, autonomy,* and *initiative.* The human newborn remains helpless longer than the young of any other species. It is in trust to the adult's competent care, and should experience no breach of basic trust.

The child needs to have an area that is really its own—just as individuals of other species need a minimum regenerative territory. The child's room should be its "autonomy area"—the new life's learning lab complete with the expendables needed for testing tension, cohesion, etc., by tensing and tearing techniques.

This leads into *initiative*—the third element of critically controlling importance during the first four years. Psychologists have long told us that children need to *touch* to get basic information. But they also need to conduct all manner of experiments, as with gravity and inertia when they knock objects off a table. Likewise, children require experiences which indicate the coherence of things. After tearing newspapers apart and finding they give poor tensional support they will want to explore silk and other materials. As W. Gray Walter has observed, "What the nervous system receives from the sense organs is information about differences—about ratios between stimuli." [8]

Children, first taking apart and then putting together, learn to coordinate spontaneously. They learn about the way Universe works.

Children mustn't be stopped thoughtlessly as they go through their basic explorations. If parents break up that exploratory initiative by too many "don'ts" or punishments, or by having things in the child's environment that are dangerous and by which the child gets hurt too frequently, spontaneity will be stifled, probably permanently. Fortunately, a few determined and reinspired

7   Erik Erikson, "Identity and the Life Cycle," *Psychological Issues,* Monograph 1 (New York: International Universities Press, 1959).

8   W. Gray Walter, *The Living Brain* (New York: Norton, 1953), p. 135.

individuals whose spontaneous employment of innate capabilities has been curtailed or abandoned due to childhood frustrations, manage to later "find" themselves, but these cases are rare.

In experimental work at Southern Illinois University, we have learned that the maturing student, like the younger learner, wants privacy—a special place. We have developed a little, individual, private room-booth with a windowed door which "belongs" to each student in our project. When the students first enter they find in their private "room" all kinds of desirable items: a telephone directly and privately connected to the teacher; a good dictionary; wall charts of the periodic table of the elements; a world globe; a wall-mounted chart of the electromagnetic spectrum; a private typewriter, and other items conducive to thought and study. It becomes an obviously realized privilege to be allowed to go into this private study, where their reflexes become progressively conditioned, by association with that environment, and the students give themselves spontaneously to study, calculation, and writing. They find themselves producing. Their minds really begin to work.

As Southern Illinois University's President Delyte Morris—a true leader—has pointed out: "The assumption here is that 'dropouts' indicate inadequacy of the educational system and not of the human individual."

In my *Ideas and Integrities*[9] I have said that education, in the sense of man's being *educente* (led out from) the monological fixations of ignorance, involves also being led into, *intro-ducente,* (introduced to) the new awareness of the dynamic fluidity of the infinite persistence of complex-yet-systematic interaction of universal principles.

I consider the primary concern of education as exploring to discover not only more about Universe and its history but also about what Universe is trying to do, about why human beings are part of it, and how they may best function in universal evolution.

9   R. Buckminster Fuller, *Ideas and Integrities* (Englewood Cliffs, N. J.: Prentice-Hall, 1963), p. 231. (Baden: Lars Müller Publishers, 2010), p. 308.—Ed.

We are finding ways to help children coordinate their spontaneous comprehension of the whole instead of becoming specialists without losing any of the advantages gained by yesterday's exclusive specialization.

Our present global civilization requires an educational approach embracing at the outset the most comprehensive review of fundamental "generalized" principles. As these are progressively mastered, the approach should continue through their subdivision and application to separate localized cases. Having established this order from "the whole to the particular" we need to take all of the advantages afforded us by the latest communications developments through which the complex patternings and behavior of Universe may be brought within reach and made part of humanity's working everyday experience.

Today, the vastness, complexity and detail of our knowledge requires restructuring into assimilable wholes, to be imparted even at the most elementary levels in terms of whole systems. We can no longer think in terms of single static entities—one thing, situation, or problem—but only in terms of dynamic changing processes and series of events that interact complexly.

Despite their venerated status, a large part, if not all of our educational institutions and their disciplines are obsolete. Virtually everything we thought we understood concerning education is fast becoming useless or worse. For example, because experiment invalidates most of the axioms of mathematics such as the existence of solids, continuous surfaces, straight lines, etc., much of the mathematical curriculum sanctioned by mathematical educators, adopted by school boards, and taught in all elementary schools is false, irrelevant, discouraging, and debilitating to the children's brain functioning.

We are going to develop an environment in which the new generation is so protected from the lovingly administered nonsense of grownups that it can develop naturally just in time to save humanity from self-annihilation.

Half a century ago, in 1917, I found myself thinking that nature didn't have separate departments of physics, chemistry, biology, and mathematics requiring meetings of department heads in order to decide how to make bubbles and roses!

I decided nature had only one department and only one arithmetical, angle-and-frequency, modulating-and-coordinating system. I am quite confident that I have discovered an importantly large area of the arithmetical, geometrical, topological, crystalographic, and energetically vectorial coordinate system employed by nature itself. It is a triangular and tetrahedronal system. It uses 60-degree coordination instead of 90-degree coordination. It permits kindergarten modeling of the fourth and fifth arithmetical powers, i.e., fourth and fifth dimensional aggregations of points and spheres, etc., in an entirely rational coordinate system. I have explored the fundamental logic of the structural mathematics strategies of nature which always employ the six sets of degrees of freedoms and most economical actions.

The omnirational coordinate system which I have named *synergetics* is not an invention. It is purely discovery. With the complete and simple modelability of synergetics it will be possible for children at home with closed-circuit TV documentaries coming to them, and making their own models, to do valid nuclear physics formulations at kindergarten age. With this fundamental structuring experience, and sensing through models, children will discover with experiments why water does what it does. They will really understand what a triangle is and what it can do and does.

I agree with Jerome Bruner, whose report of the 1959 Woods Hole Conference advanced the hypothesis that "any subject can be taught effectively in some intellectually honest form to any child at any stage of development." [10]

As Margaret Mead has indicated in her classic, *Coming of Age in Samoa,* we must direct our educational efforts to preparing

10 Jerome Bruner, *The Process of Education* (New York: Vintage, 1960), p. 33.

children for coping effectively with the choices and changes which are confronting them. We should design a *Curriculum of Change, not merely a "changing curriculum."* [11]

Obviously, one of the reasons why scientific education has seemed too difficult for many is the fact that much of its mathematics is founded upon experimentally unprovable myths which must greatly offend the intuitive sensitivity of the lucidly thinking new life.

When we combine our knowledge that the period from birth to four is the crucial "school" opportunity, with the discovery that entirely new mathematical simplicities are at hand, we must realize that educational theory is entering a period of complete revolution. Excepting the mathematical-physicists, the revolution about to take place in mathematics education may be amongst history's most violent academic *reforms*. You will not have to wait long to discover that I am right.

It is very clear to me that when children stand up, breathing and coordinating exquisitely complex patterns by themselves, get their own balance and start drinking in the patterns of cosmos and earth, they are spontaneously interested in coordinating the total information—the total stimulation. Children crave to understand—to comprehend. That is why they ask their myriad questions.

New tools will make it easier for the young to discover experimentally what really is going on in nature so that they will not have to continue taking so much nonsense on experimentally unverified axiomatic faith.

Computers, suddenly making human beings obsolete as specialists, force them back into comprehensivity functioning, which they were born spontaneously to demonstrate.

Computers as learning tools can take over much of the "educational metabolics," freeing us to really put our brains and

11 Margaret Mead, *Coming of Age in Samoa,* 14th printing (New York: Mentor, 1962), pp. 144–45. See also Alfred North Whitehead, *The Aims of Education and Other Essays* (New York: Mentor, 1951), p. 28.

wisdom to work. A recent report by the President's Science Advisory Committee recommends that the government underwrite a program to give every college student in America access to a computer by 1971. I suggest that we give every preschooler access first!

One device I have invented to provide total information integration is the "Geoscope" or miniature Earth. After sixteen years of experimentation and development, I can describe it as a 200-foot diameter sphere with 10 million electric light bulbs—each with controllable light intensity—evenly covering the entire surface and hooked up to a computer to provide, in effect, an omnidirectional spherical television tube which when seen at a distance, will have as good resolution as a fine mesh halftone print. The Geoscope, accurately picturing the whole earth, will be used to communicate phenomena presently not communicable, and therefore not comprehended by the human eye-brain relay. For example, we could show all the population data for the world for the last 300 years, identifying every 1,000 human beings by a red light located at the geographical centers occupied by each 1,000 human beings. You would then be able in one minute to develop the picture of the world's population growth and geographical spread trends of recent centuries. You would see the glowing red mass spreading northwestward around the globe like a great fire. You would be able to run that data for another second or two to carry you through three or four more decades of population growth. While the edge of the data would be unreliable, the gravity and momentum centers of population would be quite reliable. Or all the cloud cover and weather information around Earth can be shown and accelerated to predict the coming weather everywhere.

If we were to flash a red light for each 1,000 "reading problems" in U.S. urban school systems, our metropolitan areas, including the nation's capital, would flicker in distress.

According to a March 1967 *Washington Post,* "At least one out of three public school students in Washington is reading two grades or more below where he should be.... Many are reading five, six, or seven grades behind." [12]

The question I would ask of the "reading readiness" advocates is: "When are these children going to be ready to read?"

In *The Case for Early Reading,* the authors have assembled considerable and convincing evidence that preschool children [Why not call them "school-at-home" children?] want to and will learn to read at home *given the opportunity.*

Their argument that the "before-age-six" period is the *naturally* optimum time for language learning—reading included—is increasingly supported by recent research disclosures in diverse disciplines which, coupled with the historical evidence cited, merits the closest consideration.

Of current relevance is the March 1967 *NEA Journal* report of the Denver study of 4,000 school children designed to determine whether beginning reading could be taught effectively in the kindergarten.

The experimental kindergarten group who were given special reading instruction twenty minutes a day and an adjusted program in the first and later grades showed the greatest initial and long-range gains in both reading comprehension and vocabulary. They also read faster than any of the other groups at the end of the third grade. Early reading instruction was shown, in short, to have "a positive, measurable, continuing effect." [13]

Stevens and Orem would agree that kindergarten as the time for introducing reading instruction [14] is preferable to first grade. But, they argue, *prekindergarten children* must be provided an environment which epigenetically enhances early reading, for

12 Susan Filson, "Reading Levels in D.C. Schools Shock New Teachers," *Washington Post,* March 16, 1967.

13 J. Brzeinski, M. L. Harrison, and P. McKee, "Should Johnny Read in Kindergarten?" *NEA Journal,* March 1967, pp. 23–25.

14 By *instruction* they mean informal, interesting, inductive, inner-paced learning. *Auto-education* is Montessori's term.

they have the prime potential for language learning—a potential which, they say, will prove to be of revolutionary significance for educational strategists.

I am confident that these authors are going to win their "case," for it is increasingly evident that the child's neurophysiology is on their side.

What we must plan now, on an even more comprehensive scale than the important Denver project, are imaginative and innovative studies to determine the optimum school-at-home combinations of these elements: (1) home environment, with enlightened parents; (2) TV, computers, and other tools and technology conveying the most cogent content; and (3) young child's motivation and sensitive period for symbol systems mastery—and communication-computational competencies.

Another device which I have invented to encourage comprehensive thinking is my Dymaxion map, originally published in *Life,* March 22, 1943, and the first projection system to be granted a U.S. patent as a cartographic innovation. Dr. Robert Marks has described it as "the first in the history of cartography to show the whole surface of the earth in a single view with approximately imperceptible distortion of the relative shapes and sizes of the land and sea masses." [15] This map, which I now call my Sky-ocean World Map, is an aid in effectively conceiving the totality of world (and Universe) events.

Because three-fourths of Earth's surface is covered by water, I have developed a "fluid geography" approach to the study of geography, to correct the "landlubber" bias prevalent in our schools.

I have also been engaged over the years in writing a comprehensive maritime reconstruction of history—a saga of the world's sailormen "seeding" civilization by ship.

When I talk about changing obsolete, ineffective, and debilitating school patterns, the established reflexive conditioning of our

15 Robert Marks, *The Dymaxion World of Buckminster Fuller* (Carbondale, Ill.: Southern Illinois University Press, 1960), p. 49.

brains tends to expect a lag of another 100 years to bring about that change. But the rate at which information is being disseminated and integrated into our current decision-making regarding the trending topics I am discussing indicates that the changes are going to happen quite rapidly. My advice to educators who are thinking about what they may dare undertake is, "Don't hesitate to undertake the most logical solutions. *Take the biggest steps right away and you will be just on time!*"

Individuals are going to study at home in their elementary, high school, and college years. Not until their graduate-work days begin will they take residence on campus. Inasmuch as the period of greatest educational capability development is before age four the home is the primary schoolhouse—and kindergarten is the high school.

As John McHale, Executive Director of the World Resources Inventory, has noted: "It is now literally and technically possible to have the equivalent of the school (or even college) actually in the home dwelling. This may very well be the indicated direction for educational and training development in the emerging countries. It is not really a new concept. The home/family dwelling as the prime educational environ and its re-integration as a fully advantaged unit are new." [16]

One may already "tune in" on knowledge through the radio, TV, and telephone. With more sophisticated systems, now available, one may individually select, and follow through, complex sequences and instructional programs.

Advances in educational technology have now made available a number of measurably efficient, self-instructional programmed materials, which are swiftly developing into presequenced "packaged learning" devices employing video tape, film, book texts, plus the remote computer linkages via libraries and control centers.

16 John McHale, *The Ten-Year Program* (Carbondale, Ill.: Southern Illinois University, World Resources Inventory), p. 79.

As I have forecast in *Education Automation,*[17] we are faced with a future in which education will be the number one great world industry, within which will flourish an educational machine technology providing tools such as the individually selected and articulated two-way TV and an intercontinentally networked, documentaries call-up system, operative over any home two-way TV set.

In my 1938 *Nine Chains to the Moon,*[18] I outlined a number of predictions including, "Broadcast Education: the main system of general educational instruction to go on the air and screen." Frank Lloyd Wright, reviewing the book for *Saturday Review,* agreed: "Dead right. The sooner the better."[19]

With two-way TV we will develop selecting dials for the children which will not be primarily an alphabetical but rather a visual species and chronological category selecting device with secondary alphabetical subdivisions, enabling children to call up any kind of information they want about any subject and get their latest authoritative TV documentary. The answers to their questions and probings will be the best information that is available up to that minute in history.

The "lecture routine" which most teachers look forward to with as little enthusiasm as their students, will give way at all levels to the professionally best possible filmed documentaries by master teachers with hi-fi recording. Southern Illinois University's film production division at Carbondale, in collaboration with independent producer Francis Thompson, is completing a moving-picture series on my *comprehensive anticipatory, design-science explorations.*

17 R. Buckminster Fuller, *Education Automation* (Carbondale, Ill.: Southern Illinois University Press, 1962).

18 R. Buckminster Fuller, *Nine Chains to the Moon* (Philadelphia: Lippincott, 1938). Copies of the original printing (5,000) of this book are now a collector's item.—Ed. Note.

19 Frank Lloyd Wright, "Ideas for the Future," *Saturday Review,* September 17, 1938, p. 14.

While I confined my discourse to those unique aspects of my comprehensive thinking which provide pioneering interpretation of humanity's total experience as distinguished from the formally accepted and taught academic concepts, it required fifty-one hours to exhaust my inventory of unique experience interpretations and their derived patterns of generalized significance conceptionings. The fifty-one hours represented my net surviving inventory of unique thoughts which have been greatly modified and amplified by my progressive world-around university experiences.

(Over the years I have accepted more than 350 separate, unsolicited appointments or invitations to visit or revisit as a "Visiting Professor" or Lecturer at nearly 200 different universities or colleges in over thirty countries.)

Children must be allowed to discipline their own minds under the most favorable conditions—in their own special private environment. We'd better consider mass producing "one pupil schools"; that is, little well-equipped capsule rooms to be sent to all the homes; or we can design special private study rooms for homes. There are many alternatives but the traditional schoolroom is not one of them. I was invited by Einstein to meet with him and talk about one of my earlier books. I can say with authority that Einstein, when he wanted to study math and physics didn't sit in the middle of a schoolroom "desk prison." That is probably the poorest place he could have gone to study. As do any logical humans when they want to truly *study,* he went into seclusion—in his private study or laboratory.

Much of what goes on in our schools is strictly related to social experience, which, within limits, is fine. But we will be adding much more in the very near future by taking advantage of children's ability to show us what they need. When individuals are really thinking, they are tremendously isolated. They may manage to isolate themselves in an airline terminal, but it is despite the environment rather than because of it. The place to study is certainly not in a schoolroom.

The red schoolhouse—little or big—is on the way out. New educational media are making it possible to bring the most important kinds of experiences right into the home. With television reaching children in the privacy of their homes everywhere, we should bring education—school—to where the children are. This is a surprise concept—the school by television always and only in the home—if possible in a special room in the home. Ralph Waldo Emerson was right—"The household is a school of power."

TV is the number one potential emancipator from ignorance and economic disadvantage of the entire human family's residual poverty-stricken 60 percent. Even in the world's slums, TV antennas bristle. There is thus a wireless hook-up directly to the parents and children who watch their televisions avidly. Whatever comes over TV to the children and parents is the essence of education, for better or worse. What is now needed are educational TV advancements of high order.

Photographs I have taken of my grandchildren (without their awareness) as they looked at TV illustrate the fabulous concentration of the child.

Give children logical, lucid information when they want and need it, and watch them "latch on." Dr. Maria Montessori designed her "method" to tap the child's powers to attend and absorb. [20]

While great knowledge and ingenuity are being put into research on the channels through which education is conveyed, relatively little consideration has been given to *what* is conveyed in the communicated content. The magnitude of the task demands a most rigorous examination of "what" knowledge is to be imparted and in which *order, amount,* and *forms* it is to be conveyed.

So the home is the school, education is the upcoming major world industry, and TV is the great educational medium.

All of this has been made possible by *industrialization* which I define as the extracorporeal, organic, metabolic regeneration of

20 R.C. Orem, ed., *Montessori for the Disadvantaged* (New York: Putnam's, 1967).

humanity. Industrialization consists of tools, which, in turn, are externalizations of originally integral functions of humans. I divide all tools into the two main classes—*craft* tools and *industrial* tools. Craft tools consist of all those that can be invented and produced by one person starting and operating alone nakedly in the wilderness.

Industrial tools are those which cannot be produced by one person, such as the steamship *Queen Mary,* the giant dynamo, a concrete highway, New York City, or even the modern forged alloy-steel carpenter's hammer, with electro-insulated plastic handles, whose alloyed components and manufacturing operations involve thousands of people and the unique resources of several countries of Earth.

Words are the first industrial tools, for inherently they involve a plurality of people and are also inherently prior to relayed communication and integration of the respective experiences of a plurality of individuals. This is reminiscent of the scriptural account, "In the beginning was the word," which we may modify to read, "In the beginning of Industrialization was the word." Crafts are limited to a single person and involve only very local resources and very limited fragments of Earth and time, while industrialization, through the relayed experience of all people—permitted through the individualization of the spoken and written word—involves *all experiences of all people everywhere in history.*

As I stressed in my keynote address to the 1966 Music Educators' National Conference,[21] the *speech pattern of the parents* exerts a critically important formative influence during the child's early years.

21 R. Buckminster Fuller, "The Music of the New Life: Thoughts on Creativity, Sensorial Reality, and Comprehensiveness" (Keynote address presented at the National Conference on the Uses of Educational Media in the Teaching of Music, under joint auspices of the U.S. Office of Education and the Music Education National Conference, Washington, D.C., December 10, 1964). Published in the *Music Educators Journal,* part 1 (April–May 1966), part 2 (June–July 1966).

If the parents take the trouble to speak clearly, to use their language effectively, to choose appropriate words, the children are inspired to do likewise. If the parents' tones of voice are hopeful, thoughtful, tolerant, and harmonious, the children are inspired to think and speak likewise. If the parents are not parroting somebody else, but are quite clearly trying to express themselves, nothing encourages more the intuitions of the young life to commit itself not only to further exploration but to deal competently in coordinating its innate faculties. However, if the parents indicate that they are not really trying, or relapse into slang clichés, slurred mouthings, blasphemy, anger, fear, or intolerance, indicating an inferiority complex which assumes an inability of self to attain understanding by others, then the children become discouraged about their own capability to understand or to be understood.

If the proper books are on the family shelves, if there are things around the house which clearly show the children that the parents are really trying to educate themselves, then the children's confidence in family is excited and the children too try to engender the parents' confidence in their—the children's—capabilities.

The child's verbal ecological patterning is a fascinating process. My granddaughter Alexandra was born in New York. She was brought by her parents from the hospital to their apartment in Riverdale, just across from the northern end of Manhattan, which is quite a high point of land directly in the path of the take-off pattern for both of New York City's major airports, La Guardia and (now) Kennedy. The planes were going over frequently, sometimes every few seconds. There was the familiar roar and, on such a high promontory, it was a fundamental event to a new life.

The interesting result was that my granddaughter's first word was not *Mummie* or *Daddy,* but *air*—short for airplane.

How we see the world depends largely on what we are told at the outset of life before we unconsciously or subconsciously lock together our spontaneous brain reflexings.

Children can most easily learn to see things correctly only if they are spoken to intelligently right from the beginning.

As I was quoted in the *New Yorker* "Profile":

> I've made tests with children—you have to get them right
> away, before they take in too many myths. I've made a paper
> model of a man and glued him down with his feet to a globe
> of the world, and put a light at one side, and shown them
> how the man's shadow lengthens as the globe turns, until
> finally he's completely in the shadow. If you show that to
> children, they never see it any other way, and they can really
> understand how the earth revolves the sun out of sight. [22]

We are learning to test experimentally the axioms given to us as "educational" springboards, and are finding that most of the "springboards" do not spring, if they exist at all!

There is growing awareness that we have been overproducing rigorously disciplined, game-playing, scientific specialists who, through hard work and suppressed imagination, earn their academic union cards, only to have their specialized field become obsolete or by-passed swiftly by evolutionary events of altered techniques and exploratory strategies.

Biological and anthropological studies reveal that overspecialization leads to extinction. We need the philosopher-scientist-artist—the comprehensivist, not merely more deluxe-quality technician-mechanics.

Artists are now extraordinarily important to human society. By keeping their innate endowment of capabilities intact, artists have kept the integrity of childhood alive until we reached the bridge between the arts and sciences. Their greatest faculty is the ability of the imagination to formulate conceptually. Suddenly, we realize how important this conceptual capability is.

22 Quoted in Calvin Tomkins, "Profile," *New Yorker,* January 8, 1966, pp. 35–36.

Spontaneously, painters, dancers, sculptors, poets, musicians, and other artists, ask me to speak to them; or they look at my starkly scientific structures, devices, and mathematical exploration models and express satisfaction, comprehension, and enthusiasm. The miracle is that the artists are human beings whose comprehensivity was not pruned down by the well-meaning but ignorant educational customs of society.

Artists are really much nearer to the truth than have been many of the scientists.

In a beautiful demonstration, Gyorgy Kepes, of M.I.T., took uniform-size black-and-white photographs of nonrepresentational paintings by many artists. He mixed them all together with the same size of black-and-white photographs taken by scientists of all kinds of phenomena through microscopes and telescopes. He and students classified the mixed pictures by pattern types. They put round-white-glob types together—wavy-gray-line-diagonals, little circle types, etc. together. When so classified and hung, one could not distinguish between the artist's works and scientific photographs taken through instruments. What was most interesting was that if you looked on the backs of the pictures you could get the dates and the identities. Frequently the artist had conceived of the pattern or parts in infra- or ultravisible realms. The conceptual capability of the artists' intuitive formulation of the evolving new by subconscious coordinations are tremendously important. Science has begun to take a new view of the artist.

Philip Morrison, Head of Cornell's department of nuclear physics, talks about what he terms "right-hand" and "left-hand" sciences. Right-hand science deals in all the proven scientific formulas and experiments, while left-hand science deals in all of the as-yet unknown or unproven, that is, with all it is going to take intellectually, intuitively, speculatively, imaginatively, and even mystically, by inspired persistence, to open up the as-yet unknown.

We have been governmentally underwriting only the right-hand science, making it bigger and sharper. How could Congress justify appropriations of billions for dreams?

Pride, fear, economic and social insecurity, and the general reluctance of humanity to let go of nonsense in order vastly to reorganize are basic to the problem of education.

We adults must learn about our universe and how to modify the environment in order to permit life to operate and articulate the innate capabilities of humanity, the range and richness of which we are only beginning to apprehend. Innate cerebral and metaphysical capabilities have been frustrated by negative factors of the environment—not the least of which are the people in it who surround every individual. Today, the young people really want to know about things, they want to get closer to the truth, and my job is to do all I can to help them.

What I describe as *positive design-science reformations of the environment* must now be undertaken with the intent of permitting our innate faculties and facilities to be realized with subconscious coordinations of our organic process. *Reform of the environment* undertaken to defrustrate our innate capabilities, whether the frustration be caused by the inadequacies of the physical environment or by the debilitating reflexes of other humans, will *permit* humanity's original, innate capabilities to become successful. *Politics and conventionalized education have sought erroneously to mold or reform humanity, i.e., the collective individual.*

I have thought long and hard about architectural education and its potential for promoting environmental reform. I envision an utterly revised education of the architect, enabling successful students to operate on their own initiative in dealing both comprehensively and in effective depth in mathematics, chemistry, physics, biology, geology, industrial tooling, network systems, economics, law, business administration, medicine, astronautics, computers, general systems theory, patents, and the whole gamut of heretofore highly specialized subjects.

This "comprehensivity curriculum" will prepare the graduating architects to gain the design initiative, performing thereafter not as economic slaves of technically illiterate clients and patron despots but as comprehensivists, integrating and developing the significance of all the information won by all the respective disciplines of the specialized sciences and humanities, converting this information into technical advantages for world society in completely tooled-up and well-organized comprehensive anticipatory *livingry systems*.

When President Eisenhower was first confronted by the strategic data on atomic warfare he said, "There is no alternative to peace," without defining the latter or indicating how it could be secured. Professor John Platt, Chicago University physicist and biophysicist, in a thorough survey of the overall shapes of a family of trend curves which comprehensively embrace science, technology, and humanity in Universe, said in 1964, "The World has become too dangerous for anything less than Utopia," but did not suggest how it might be attained. Jerome Wiesner, head of the department of nuclear physics at M.I.T. and past science adviser to Presidents Kennedy and Johnson, wrote in a recent issue of the *Scientific American* that "the clearly predictable course of the arms race is a steady downward spiral into oblivion."

So far, the only known and feasible means of arresting that spiral, by elimination of the cause of war, is the program of the World Students Design Decade. This ten-year plan of world architectural students is divided into five evolutionary stages of two years each. Phase One, "World Literacy Regarding World Problems," was on exhibit in the Tuileries Garden in Paris, France, for the first ten days of July 1965 (under the auspices of the International Union of Architects' Eighth World Congress). Emphasizing the central function of education and communication in overall planning, it dramatized the need for an informed world society to cope with the global nature of our problems.

It confronted the world with those basic facts leading the students to the research conclusion that human survival apparently depends upon an immediate, consciously coordinated, world-around, computerized, research marshalling and inception of the theoretically required additional inventions and industrial network integrations for the swiftest attainment and maintenance of physical success of all humanity.

Phase Two, "Prime Movers and Prime Metals," focusing upon the design of more efficient energy and metals utilization, was exhibited with the "Tribune Libre" section of the Ninth World U.I.A. Congress in Prague, Czechoslovakia, June–July 1967.

There is a new dedication on the part of the world's young. Students are corresponding with each other all over the globe. These young people are about to seize the initiative, to help us make humanity a success on Earth.

What I call "The Third Parent"—TV—is bringing babies half-hourly world news as well as much grownup-authored, discrediting drivel. The students in revolt on the university campus are the first generation of TV-reared babies. They insist on social justice the world around. They sense that imminent change is inexorable.

On Southern Illinois University's Carbondale campus, we are setting up a great computer program to include the many variables now known to be operative in world-around industrial economics. In the machine's memory bank, we will store all the basic data such as the "where" and "how much" of each class of physical resources; location of the world's people; trendings and important needs of humanity, etc.

Next, we will set up a computer feeding game, called "How to Make the World Work." We will bring people from all over the world to start playing the game relatively soon. There will be competitive teams from all around Earth, testing their theories on how to make the world work. If a team resorts to political pressures to accelerate their advantages and are not able to wait for the going gestation rates to validate their theory, they are apt to be in trouble. When you get into politics, you are very liable to get into war. War is the ultimate tool of politics. If war develops, the side inducing it loses the game.

Essence of "success in making the world work" will be to make *all* people able to become world citizens free to enjoy the whole Earth, going wherever they want at any time, able to take care of all the needs of all their forward days without any interference with any other person and never at the cost of another person's equal freedom and advantage.

I think that the communication task of reporting on the computerized playing of the game "How to Make the World Work" will become extremely popular all around Earth. We're going to be playing the game soon at S.I.U., and you'll be hearing more about it!

So, 1967 is the year of *The Case for Early Reading.*

Fortunately, the authors did not wait for "official permission" to use their initiative in exploring innovative approaches to answering the question: "When and under what circumstances should reading instruction begin?"

No one licensed the inventors of the airplane, telephone, electric light, and radio to go to work. It took only five men to invent these world transforming developments. The license comes only from the blue sky of the inventor's intellect.

The individual intellect disciplinedly paces the human individual, who disciplinedly paces science. Science disciplinedly paces technology by expanding the limits of technical, advantage-generating knowledge. Technology paces industry by progressively increasing the range and velocity inventory of technical capabilities. Industry in turn paces economics by continually altering and accelerating the total complex of environment controlling capabilities of man. Economics paces the everyday evolution acceleration of man's affairs. The everyday patterning evolution poses progressively accelerating problems regarding the understanding of the new relative significance of our extraordinarily changing and improving degrees of relative advantage in controlling our physical survival and harmonic satisfaction.

In 1927, I gave up forever society's general economic dictum that every individual who wants to survive must earn a living, substituting instead a search for the tasks that needed to be done that no one else was doing or attempting to do, which if accomplished, would physically and economically advantage society and eliminate pain.

By disciplining my faculties, I was able, as an individual, to develop technical and scientific capability to invent the physical innovations and their service industry logistics.

Seventeen of my prime inventions in a wide range of categories have been granted a total of 145 patents in fifty-six countries around the world; incidentally, these patents in late years have produced millions of dollars of revenue. There are over 200 licensees, a number of which are industrial "blue chip" corporations, operating under these patents.

I've never had an "expert" who ever comprehended in significant degree the importance of any new development on which I was working. While this is deplorable, it's also understandable in the big corporations because research and engineering heads, confronted with something from the "outside," become very defensive, believing that acquiescence or approval would imply an admission that they are not alert themselves. [23]

1967 is also the year of Canada's World's Fair, EXPO 67; the United States Pavilion is a 250-foot diameter Geodesic Skybreak Bubble. [24] I invented the geodesic dome in 1947, and today can

23 See "Creativity Innovation, and the Condition of Man," a dialogue between R. Buckminster Fuller and Stanley Foster Reed, *Employment Service Review,* Washington, D.C., March–April 1967.

24 David Jacobs, "An Expo Named Buckminster Fuller," *New York Times Magazine,* April 23, 1967, pp. 32–33.

count over 6,000 of my structures in fifty countries,[17] ranging from play domes to the 384-foot diameter dome which rose in Baton Rouge, Louisiana, as the largest clear span enclosure in history.

A U.S. government citation describes "air deliverable geodesic structures" as the "first basic improvement in mobile environmental control in 2,600 years." I can assure you I have never waited for any Bureau of Breakthroughs to grant me my permit to ponder, produce, or prognosticate.

Forty years ago, after my pioneering studies had revealed the low technical advance in everyday dwelling facilities as compared with transport and communication developments, I invented my 1927 Dymaxion[25] House to function as part of my concept of an air-deliverable, mass-producible world-around, new human life protecting and nurturing, scientific dwelling service industry to transfer high scientific capability from a weaponry to livingry focus.

Children, born truthful, learn deception and falsehood from their elders' prohibition of truth. Much of this prohibition arises from a great, largely unconscious, parental selfishness born of drudgery and dissatisfaction (visibly rampant in the slums). The housing of children during their upbringing is the fundamental function of the home. If we solve the problem of the home, we can erase much of this unenlightenment.

The same year (1927), I published my conviction that two billion new era premium technology-dwelling devices would be needed before 2000 A.D., requiring a whole new world-encompassing service industry. I predicted it would take twenty-five years to establish that new industry. In 1952, right on theoretical schedule, the Ford Motor Company purchased the first of my large geodesic domes, which are the prototypes of the new era premium technology structures.

25 Dymaxion: The maximum gain of advantage from the minimal energy output.

17 See note 6, p. 42.

I anticipate that full scale industrialization of the livingry service industry will be realized by 1977, or just 60 years after the model "T" inaugurated the major world mass-production industry. Henry Ford, Sr., pioneered the long-range, world-around historical development of the application of the tools-to-make-tools system of mass production to larger end-product tools, with his motorized road vehicle in 1907.

My structures, as reported in engineering and scientific publications, can cover very large clear span spaces more economically than by any other rectilinear or other shaped systems—for example, 1,000-fold more economically weightwise than accomplished by the dome of St. Peter's in Rome, or thirty times more efficiently than by reinforced concrete.

The New York Herald Tribune in February 1962 reported that Dr. Home of Cambridge University had announced, at a world conference of molecular biologists, the discovery of the generalized principles governing the protein shells of the viruses. "All these virus structures had proved to be geodesic spheres of various frequencies. The scientists reported that not only were the viruses geodesic structures, which latter had been discovered earlier by Buckminster Fuller, but also that the mathematics which apparently controls nature's formulations of the viruses had also been discovered (1933) and published by Fuller a number of years earlier (1944).[26]

Although the words "genius" and "creativity" have been employed to explain my being "well known," I am convinced that the only reason I am known at all is because I set about deliberately in 1927 to be a comprehensivist in an era of almost exclusive trending and formal disciplining toward specialization. Inasmuch as everyone else was becoming a specialist, I didn't have any competition whatsoever. I was such an antithetical standout that whatever I did became prominently obvious, therefore, "well known."

26 R. Buckminster Fuller, "Conceptuality of Fundamental Structures," in *Structure in Art and in Science*, ed. Gyorgy Kepes (New York: George Braziller, 1965), p. 76.

Luckily, as a special student at the United States Naval Academy in 1917, I had been exposed to a comprehensive educational strategy fundamentally different from the then-prevailing ivy-league model. The potential I have since developed, every physically normal child also has at birth.

What, if anything, is hopeful about my record is that I am an average human and therefore whatever I have been able to accomplish also can be accomplished, and probably better, by average humanity, each successive generation of which has less to unlearn.

Humanity is beginning to transform from being utterly helpless and only subconsciously coordinate with important evolutionary events. We have gotten ourselves into much trouble, but at the critical transformation stage we are reaching a point where we are beginning to make some measurements—beginning to know a little something. We are probably coming to the first period of direct consciously assumed responsibility of humanity in Universe.

Human beings sort, classify, and order in direct opposition to entropy—which is the law of increase of the random element—increase of disorder. Human beings sort and classify internally and subconsciously as well as externally and consciously, driven by intellectual curiosity and brain. Human beings seem to be the most comprehensive anti-entropy[18] function of Universe.

Human beings, as designed, are obviously intended to be a success just as the hydrogen atom is designed to be a success. The fabulous ignorance of humanity and our long-wrongly conditioned reflexes have continually allowed the new life to be impaired, albeit lovingly and unwittingly.

Our most important task is to become as comprehensive as possible by intellectual conviction and "self-debiasing," not through ignorant yielding, but through a progressively informed displacement of invalid assumptions and dogma by discovery of the valid

---

18 Fuller later adopted the word *syntropy* as the complementary principle to *entropy*.

data. In this development, the young will lead the old in swiftly increasing degree. The child is the trim tab of the future. Let us respect in our children the profound contribution trying to emerge. The Bible was right: "...and a little child shall lead them."

As one who has spent his own lifetime comprehensively *putting things together* in an age of specialized *taking apart*—as a poet—I close with these lines—

And with Industrialization a uniformly beautiful
world race emerges
as does the fine chiseled head
from the rough marble block
certifying the god-like untrammeled beauty
of a perfect human process
implicit in the dynamic designing
genius of the mind.... [27]

27 R. Buckminster Fuller, *Untitled Epic Poem on the History of Industrialization* (Highlands, N.C.: Jonathan Williams, Publisher, 1962), p. 116.

Heartbeats and Illions

Scientists who know the sun is not "going down" "see" it setting. Scientists who know there are no solids, or straight lines, or things still "see" and talk about solids, straight lines, and things (e.g., they refer to high-energy events as "particles"). Humanity's intellect and sensorial reflexes are completely uncoordinated. We see clouds floating by, birds flying, and people moving, but we can't see plants or humans growing. We can't see the economic charts realistically: humanity gets out of the way only when it sees the motion. We cannot see the dates on the calendar moving nor the hour or minute hands on the clock moving; we can only see the second hand move. Like parrots, we learn to recite numbers without any sensorial appreciation of their significance. We have yielded so completely to specialization that we disregard the comprehensive significance of information.

Human beings' faulty number sense is being further confused by meaningless money magnitudes—for instance, the combined war budgets of the United States, NATO, China, and Russia, which annually average about $200 billion.[19] People talk about these cost magnitudes without any sensorial identity of relative significances. Dollar bills are approximately seven inches long by three

March 1973. Originally published in *World* magazine in two parts. See background on chapter 1, p. 27.

19 According to the Stockholm International Peace Research Institute (SIPRI), global military expenditures and the arms trade were estimated to be $1.46 trillion in 2008, up 4 percent from 2007. *SIPRI Yearbook 2009 Armaments, Disarmament and International Security* (Oxford, 2008), http://www.sipri.org/yearbook/2009/05 (accessed September 3, 2009).

inches wide. If we stack them and glue their edges together, as with a pad of paper, we get approximately $200 in each one inch of stacking. If we keep adding to the pile, it forms a column whose cross section is approximately three inches by seven inches. As we keep on adding to it, it gets too high to be stable, so we rotate it from the vertical to horizontal. It will begin to look like a beam, a seven-inch-by-three-inch beam. The lumber business has beam framings called four-by-eights. Finished by planing, this prime lumber size dresses out at three inches by seven inches, but is still called four-by-eight. So our structural four-by-eight of laminated dollar bills, when extended to ten feet in length, has the shape of a beam, such as you may see in short ceiling spans of any wood-framed house. So we have now a floor beam of solidly laminated dollar bills. We keep adding more bills to both ends of this four-by-eight until it consists of 200 billion one-dollar bills. Such a four-by-eight of 200 billion one-dollar bills will circle right around Earth at approximately 40 degrees north latitude running due east and west through New York, Pittsburgh, St. Louis, Kansas City, San Francisco, Tokyo, Peking, Istanbul, Madrid, the Azores, and back to New York.

That we are spending $200 billion annually to get ready to destroy one another gives you an idea of how "magnitude ignorant" and "sense-disconnected" humanity is; when it says, "we can't *afford* to take proper care of the majority of world people," while plowing food back to raise prices to make money, and simultaneously raising tariffs to discourage production by other peoples around the Earth. We humans need to find a means of cerebrating a little more realistically about number significance and about what we have learned about the principles governing eternally regenerative Universe—and our tiny planet and its ecologically regenerative system, which has no sovereign boundaries nor rent bills due to our planetary landlord, the sun, who might shut off our life support because we say we can't afford to pay that cosmic bill.

We need a way for humans to coordinate their senses and thought in terms of their personal life experience, for instance, with their respective allotments of life time. Each one is born to some average total lifetime expectancy, as calculated from census statistics by the life insurance-company mathematics. Some Russians live 150 years, but the average in the Western world is now about 70 years,[20] having doubled in the last three-quarters of a century. Let us think, then, about the minutes and seconds you and I really have at our elective disposal out of every twenty-four hours. We all have to sleep—about one-third of our time. A lot of our time is dedicated to just going from here to there. We don't have very much available to us for elective investment. The one kind of time measurement directly and sensorially available to all of us is our heart beating. We have a built-in clock. Just close your eyes lying in bed, and feel your own pulse or heartbeat. Healthy hearts beat between sixty and one hundred times each minute; you're quite normal if you are pulsing sixty to the minute, or *once each second* of Earth revolution time. So a *one-second-of-time* heartbeat is a natural-time increment that you can really feel. Let us now assess human history and Universe in one-second heartbeats. For instance, two weeks is 1 million heartbeats. One year is only 31 million heartbeats. You enter college at 500 million heartbeats. At the prime of life, i.e., about thirty-two years of age, you've had about 999 million heartbeats. So not until you start the second half of your life do you need to get into billions magnitude. Vitally speaking then, millions are large numbers. The money game of "millions" and those who are millionaires have led us to assume that millions are inferior magnitudes leading swiftly to eccentric

20 The average life expectancy for the total world population in 2009 is 66.57 years. Japan has the highest of the G-8 countries and large industrialized countries, with a life expectancy of 82.12 (3rd of all countries behind only Macau and Andorra). The life expectancies for the other G-8 countries are: Canada, 81.23 (8th overall); France, 80.98 (9th); Germany, 79.26 (32nd); Italy, 80.20 (19th); Russia, 66.03 (162nd); the U.K., 79.01 (36th); and the U.S., 78.11 (50th). CIA, *The World Factbook 2009* (Washington, DC, 2009), https://www.cia.gov/library/publications/the-world-factbook/rankorder/2102rank.html (accessed September 5, 2009).

billionaires. If you live to full life insurance "expectancy"—seventy years—you will complete only 2 billion heartbeats. If you reach 100 years, you've had only 3 billion heartbeats. Christ and Mohammed both lived tens of billions of heartbeats ago. The *billions* magnitude does not exhaust itself rapidly. You may begin to realize how preposterous it is that humanity is spending $200 billion each year on armaments on the erroneous assumption that we cannot afford to support all humanity, when that magnitude of 200 *billion,* considered in your own heartbeats, takes history back to the dawning of the 8,000-years-ago earliest-known Egyptian people. The earliest known artifacts of artistically cultured people were being fashioned only 500 billion heartbeats, i.e., 15,000 years ago in northeast Thailand. We don't exhaust *billion* magnitudes until we go back historically to 30,000 years ago, about the time of the last ice age. Earlier than that we must go for the first time into the *trillion* magnitudes. The earliest known skull of a human being found by the Leakey father-and-son team was in live use 2.5 million years ago, which is only 75 trillion heartbeats ago. The capital worth in tools and other resources of all the nations of the Earth in 1972 is also estimated to be 75 trillion U.S. dollars, which last year yielded the annual world income of $3.6 trillion. Heartbeat magnitudes give us an idea of the nonsense characterizing the reflexing of human brains when talking "dollars." As the $75 trillion worth of the world's organized wealth-regenerating capacity is just about the same number as the number of heartbeats-ago of the earliest known humans on Earth—2.5 million years ago—it suggests that during each one-second heartbeat of that time humans were making and "saving" $1 net.

They were, in fact, saving memories of experience, which ever multiply, from which accumulate metaphysical know-how that has never been entered into the ledgers of world-wealth accounting. Those pages are preoccupied only with sovereignty-guaranteed, physical-property equities of socialist or capitalist governments and the economic enterprises that they respectively foster. GNP stands for gross national product annually. GWP stands for gross world product annually, the GWP of 1972 estimated at $3.6 trillion.[21] The world's population of 1972 was $3\frac{2}{3}$ billion humans.[22] A trillion is 1,000 billion; therefore, the world's 1972 GWP of $3.6 trillion meant an average income for each world human of $1,000. However, the production was not evenly distributed, as is well known, and half the world's people averaged an income of $2,000 each, while the other half averaged $100 each.[23] In 1810, just before industrialization began in the United States, the annual individual income was less than the $100-annual-income purchasing capability of the 1972 world's industrial-as-yet-have-nots. The difference is the spread of the new method of survival by industrial rather than by farm and craft means. The curve of this rising number of highly advantaged humans shows less than 1 percent benefited haves as of 1900, 4 percent haves as of the entry into World War I, and 20 percent haves as of entry into World War II. In 1972 we went through the 50 percent haveness point.[24] Nineteen hundred and seventy-three opens the new chapter of

21 The estimated GWP in 2008 was $62.25 trillion. CIA, *The World Factbook 2009* (Washington, DC, 2009), https://www.cia.gov/library/publications/the-world-factbook/geos/xx.html (accessed September, 3 2009).

22 The world population in 2009 is 6.83 billion, according to the Population Division of the Department of Economic and Social Affairs of the United Nations Secretariat. *World Population Prospects: The 2008 Revision; Highlights* (New York, 2009).

23 Today's global development community distinguishes between four fundamental standards of living: "extreme poverty," "moderate poverty," "middle income," and "high income." "Extreme poverty" is defined as the inability to "meet basic needs for survival," living on less than $1 per day per person. "Moderate poverty" means, "basic needs are just barely met," living on between $1 and $2 per day per person (not the same as "relative poverty" in wealthy countries). "Middle income" indicates "incomes of a few thousand per year" (not the same measures of "middle income" in wealthy countries); and "high income" is above that. By those definitions, in 2001 the percentage of humanity in poverty dropped to 44% (2.7 of 6.1 billion): 1.1 billion in extreme poverty and 1.6 billion in moderate poverty. Jeffrey Sachs, *The End of Poverty: Economic Possibilities for our Time* (New York, 2005), chapter 1; and S. Chen and M. Ravallion, "How Have the World's Poorest Fared Since the Early 1980s?" World Bank Policy Research Working Paper 3341, June 2004.

24 See note 11, p. 94.

human history wherein, for the first time, *the majority of humanity are haves*. For the 2.5 million years of man's known presence on Earth, a majority of 99 percent were have-nots subsisting at or below the living standards of the half of humanity who in 1972 received only $ 100 of the gross world product. Nineteen hundred and seventy-two was history's most critical year, when the sudden avalanche of new affluence left the not-as-yet-industrialized have-nots dramatically dismayed by the differences in human fortune.

Up to 1972 the ever-increasing irritation of the majority of human have-nots continually multiplied the probability of world revolution. Up to 1972 this could have brought holocaust so devastating as to preclude the further existence of any human beings on our planet at any standard of living. There is now the possibility that the majority of humans who are now haves will realize increasingly that they cannot enjoy their haveness while the dismay and irritability of the have-nots persists. The haves will come to understand that it is now highly feasible for the first time in history to accelerate the realization of 100 percent haveness—this realization to be reached at the earliest by 1985, a time when the majority of all present humanity will still be alive and young enough to enjoy the new concept—by then the established norm—of human beings as cosmically designed to be *successful* in Universe, even as are the chemical elements and the principles of radiation and gravity.

At the present time the $ 200 billion going for armaments [25] of all the great powers of Earth is a little more than goes to feed the 1.8 billion $ 100-a-year have-nots.

Allowing three years for this to make sense and get going, it also happens to be true that the same $ 200 billion annually appropriated by world governments for military use will purchase the 40 million new $ 5,000 homes required annually during each of the next twenty-five years until A.D. 2000 if we are to accommodate those now ill-housed as well as the interim world-population increase.

---

25 See note 19, p. 139.

Next we get into the *quadrillion* magnitudes to express the probable age of our planet Earth, whose birth was only 100 quadrillion heartbeats ago. [26] Then we come to the age of Universe thus far known to have existed, which is only 300 quadrillion heart-beats ago. We don't know of anything older than 300 quadrillion heartbeats ago. At this historical moment, the limit of anything we can talk about observationally as time is only 300 quadrillion heartbeats ago.

Let us now consider how fast the fastest-known phenomenon can travel in our shortest sensory-time interval—a one-second heartbeat. This fastest-known-in-Universe speed is the 186,000 miles traveled by light and all other electromagnetic radiation in one heartbeat of time.

Satisfactorily generated and transmitted, electric light pulses cyclically and appears as steady, or constant, light. The cyclically pulsing light occurs at sixty pulses per second of Earth-rotation time, which is also about sixty pulses per heartbeat. This is because we also see pulsatively, in sixty separate light takes per each one-second heartbeat. We see at a rate of heartbeats^2 (heartbeats to the second power; don't say heartbeats "squared" [27]). For a sequence of motion-picture film frames to appear faultlessly as "motion" to our eyes, the optimum speed is twenty-four frames per second. The difference between the sixty per second, eye-take cycling is due to the after-image clear-away lag.

When the adult human male hand is placed palm down against a firm surface, the thickness of the widest part of the thumb's first joint is approximately one inch. The distance from the tip of the

26 The world is now thought to be about 4.55 billion years old, just about one-third of the 13.7-billion-year age estimated for the universe. CIA, *The World Factbook 2009* (Washington, DC, 2009), https://www.cia.gov/library/publications/the-world-factbook/geos/xx.html (accessed September 3, 2009).

27 Fuller is making reference to his view that since triangles, just as squares, can be subdivided to illustrate "second-powering" (i.e., $2^2 = 4$, $3^2 = 9$, $4^2 = 16$, etc.), our terminology should not be skewed toward a "rectilinear" language. See also note 34, p. 172.

adult male's pointing (or index) finger to that finger's first knuckle is also one inch. You don't have to say "approximately" one inch, because an inch is an approximation as are all measures, as Heisenberg's "indeterminism" made clear. An adult human foot length is twelve inches. Three "feet" make one adult male's stride of one yard, i.e., thirty-six inches. An "extra long" stride is approximately one meter, or thirty-nine inches plus.

There are, of course, much smaller humanly visible distance increments than an inch, for instance a hair's breadth, this being approximately the same as the smallest interval visible to the naked eye, which is approximately one-hundredth of one inch. At one-hundredth of an inch, the white spaces between dark points on a measuring scale blur together, as do the separate "dots" in "halftone," black-and-white printed pictures. At a two-hundredth-of-an-inch interval between the separately colored dots of printing, the optical illusion seems "absolutely true to nature."

The smallest-known orderly phenomenon in Universe is the atom. The diameter of the atom's nucleus is the smallest-known distance measurement in Universe. The diameter of the outer shell of the atom is approximately 10,000 times that of its nuclear diameter. The ratio of diameter sizes of the atomic nucleus and the diameter of its outer electron orbit (shell) is 1 to 10,000. This also is somewhat the same order of magnitude as is the 8,000-mile diameter of Earth in relation to its own sun-orbiting diameter of 184 million miles, i.e., 1 to 23,000. But Earth is not the solar system's nucleus. The sun is the planetary nucleus. Earth orbits the sun at a diameter that is only 230 times the diameter of the sun. Pluto, however, is the outermost-known planet, ergo, it is the sun-nucleated system's outer-shell-describing planet, and Pluto's orbital diameter is 9,000 times the diameter of the sun. Thus, the solar system discloses approximately the same nucleus-to-shell diameters ratio as that of the atoms, and may indeed do so exactly, for there are new calculations suggesting a tenth planet at possibly the exact 10,000-sun-diameter's distance.

As companion to our one-second heartbeat as the unit of time, we will now adopt the diameter of the nucleus of the atom as our experiential *unit of minimum distance,* or space measurement. Science uses the diameter of the outer orbital "shell" of the atom as its unit of space measuring, and calls that atomic-shell diameter one angstrom unit. One angstrom is the diameter of the spherical domain of one atom, and it is 10,000 atomic-nucleus diameters.

Ten billion angstroms equal one meter in space (or distance measuring), which is about 3 ⅓ feet. So one meter is 100 trillion nuclear diameters, i.e., 10,000 times 10 billion. There are 1,600 meters in a mile. This means that there are 160 quadrillion nuclear diameters in a mile. Here we have again reached the quadrillion magnitude, which number accommodated the total number of heartbeats in the age of the thus-far discovered Universe.

Astronomers deal in light-years as their units of distance in space. One light-year is the distance radiation light travels in any one linear direction within one Earth-around-sun-orbiting year. Light travels at a rate of 186,000 miles a second, which is 6 trillion miles in one light-year. Multiplying 6 trillion miles per year by the 160 quadrillion atomic-nuclear diameters in a mile, we find that light travels in one year a distance of 96 octillion nuclear diameters (96×10^{28}). With the world's most powerful telescope—the 200-inch reflector at Mount Palomar—the diameter of the total sphere of observation of our Universe in all directions thus far explored by Earth's astronomers is 22 billion light-years, [28] which is 22 duodecillion atomic nucleus diameters = 2×10^{40}. And that is as big and as little and as long ago as we now can go.

---

28 Numerous telescopes of newer technology and design are now more powerful than the one at Mount Palomar. Significantly expanding the 11-billion-light-year-radius sweep-out when this article was written, an object, named GRB 090423, was found by NASA's Swift satellite on April 23, 2009. The Harvard Smithsonian Center for Astrophysics issued a press release stating that their astronomers, "along with colleagues elsewhere in the United States and the United Kingdom, have discovered the most distant object in the universe—a spectacular stellar explosion known as a gamma-ray burst located about 13 billion light years away." Center for Astrophysics, "Press Release No. 2009-11," http://www.cfa.harvard.edu/news/2009/pr200911.html (accessed July 14, 2009).

We are not familiar with the Greek or Latin number prefixes like *dec-, non-,* or *oct-* of these larger numbers, nowadays spoken of by the scientist only as *powers of ten* (see table); but on the other hand, we are indeed familiar with the Anglo-American words *one, two, three,* wherefore we may prefix these more familiar designations to the constant *illion* suffix, which we will now always equate with a set of three successive zeros.

We used to call 1,000 *one thousand;* we will now call it 1-illion. Each additional set of three zeros is recognized by the prefixed number of such three-zero sets: 1 million = 2-illion; 1 billion is 3-illion (always hyphenated to avoid confusion with the set of subillion enumerators, i.e., 206 4-illions). The English identified illions only with six zero additions, while the Americans used illions for every three zeros, starting, however, only *after 1,000,* overlooking its three zeros as common to all of them. Both the English and American systems were thus forced to use awkward nomenclature by retaining the initial word *thousand*, as belonging to a different concept and a historically earlier time. Using our consistent illion nomenclature, we express the largest experientially conceivable measurement, which is the diameter of thus-far observed Universe measured in diameters of the nucleus of the atom, and that measurement is a neat 20 13-illions.

The numbers traffic in entirely nonsensorially geared terms helps to produce such misconceptions as that of our Earth standing still and the rest of Universe revolving around it, with the stars considered by most to be some kind of "side show." The non-sensorially identified number reflexing permits the President of the United States publicly to congratulate the astronauts about going *up* to the moon and back *down* to Earth—when Universe has no up and down—with few of his listeners aware of the manifest ignorance. That humans have made a number of successful trips to the moon despite such ignorance discloses the excellence of the instrumentation involved; for we heard the scientists at

Houston talking back and forth to the astronauts about the speeds at which their rocketed capsule was traveling through space, and the speeds given were relative to both the moon and Earth standing still in space. All the while, however, Earth and its Earth-orbiting moon and the moon capsule were traveling around the sun at 60,000 mph. This should have been added to the 5–15,000 mph of the astronauts' reported speed. But that is not all, for in addition to our 60,000 mph around the sun, the sun itself and its nine planets are traveling as a team both within and with the fat-centered, thin-edged, disk-shaped galactic system, the rim of which we call the Milky Way. Our sun and its planets are traveling in their flight-holding position about three-quarters out from the center of the galactic system, which is merry-go-rounding in the cosmos with its perimeter revolving at 1 million mph. Where we in the sun group are co-traveling, the galactic merry-go-round is revolving at 800,000 mph; that's another 800,000 mph to be added to the 60,000 mph Earth and moon are traveling around the sun, all to be added to the little 5–15,000 mph reported to us over TV by the Houston space-center scientists as the speed that the Earth-to-moon capsule was making. That we are so self-deceived and so careless in accounting our experiences renders absurd all would be serious discussions of wealth, financial equities, and "costs" in general.

Up to the twentieth century, "reality" was everything humans could touch, smell, see, and hear. Since the initial publication of the chart of the electro-magnetic spectrum in 1930, humans have learned that what they can touch, smell, see, and hear is less than one-millionth of reality. Ninety-nine percent of all that is going to affect our tomorrows is being developed by humans using instruments and working in the ranges of reality that are non-humanly sensible.

Let's take another look at ourselves. Although our planet seems so huge to us that we see it as stretching away to infinity in all directions, it is only 8,000 miles in diameter. Our highest mountain's altitude is five miles; our deepest ocean's depth, five miles. Ten miles is the maximum spherical radius aberration of our planet's surface. Ten miles in relation to the 8,000-mile diameter of the Earth is 1/800. A twelve-inch steel ball, polished mirror smooth, may have visually undetectable aberrations greater than that 1/800 of its diameter. The highest mountain and deepest ocean differential of Earth is invisible on a twelve-inch globe. It is equally invisible to the astronauts on the moon, or at any distance away from Earth. Humans average about five feet tall. There are about 5,000 feet to a mile, so a thousand humans standing on one another's heads reach a mile high. Ten thousand humans standing on one another's heads equal the difference between Earth's highest mountain and its deepest ocean. We've found that difference to be invisible, so you and I are 1/10,000 invisible in respect to our planet.

The 8,000-mile-diameter Earth is about 1/100 the diameter of the sun. A one-inch-diameter wire circle held at arm's length is congruent with the apparent disk of the sun seen through the clouds. One-hundredth of an inch is practically invisible to the unaided human eye: Earth at best is a tiny speck on the disk of the sun. The sun is 92 million miles away, and the next nearest star, Rigel Kent,[29] is 270,000 times farther away than the sun; it is 25 trillion miles away from Earth. We are getting all our biological life support on Earth by radio from the sun. And the sun is a very small star; i.e., the 200 million-mile diameter of Betelgeuse, in the constellation Orion, has a circumference bigger than the orbit of Earth around the sun.[30] There are more than 100 billion stars in our galaxy, which is an average galaxy star population. And

---

29 The next nearest star is now considered to be Proxima Centauri, which is 4.2 light years from Earth—in cosmic terms, nearly 25 trillion miles away from Earth. *Norton's Star Atlas and Reference Handbook*, 20th Ed. (New York, 2003), p. 112.

---

30 The most recent calculations put the diameter of Betelgeuse at approximately 465 million miles, almost as large as the orbit of Jupiter around the Sun. University of California at Berkeley, "Press Release," June 9, 2009, http://berkeley.edu/news/media/releases/2009/06/09_betelim.shtml (accessed September 3, 2009).

Number of zeros	Power of ten	American system	British system	Dymaxion system [31]
3	10^3	Thousand	Thousand	One-Illion
6	10^6	Million	Million	Two-Illions
9	10^9	Billion	Milliard	Three-Illions
12	10^{12}	Trillion	Billion	Four-Illions
15	10^{15}	Quadrillion	−	Five-Illions
18	10^{18}	Quintillion	Trillion	Six-Illions
21	10^{21}	Sextillion	−	Seven-Illions
24	10^{24}	Septillion	Quadrillion	Eight-Illions
27	10^{27}	Octillion	−	Nine-Illions
30	10^{30}	Nonillion	Quintillion	Ten-Illions
33	10^{33}	Decillion	−	Eleven-Illions
36	10^{36}	Undecillion	Sextillion	Twelve-Illions
39	10^{39}	Duodecillion	−	Thirteen-Illions
42	10^{42}	Tredecillion	Septillion	Fourteen-Illions
45	10^{45}	Quattuordecillion	−	Fifteen-Illions
48	10^{48}	Quindecillion	Octillion	Sixteen-Illions
51	10^{51}	Sexdecillion	−	Seventeen-Illions
54	10^{54}	Septendecillion	Nonillion	Eighteen-Illions
57	10^{57}	Octodecillion	−	Nineteen-Illions
60	10^{60}	Novemdecillion	Decillions	Twenty-Illions

Significant numbers, one nuclear diameter taken as unit measurement

One-illion	1×10^4	One angstrom in atomic nuclei diameters
Three-illions	1×10^{10}	Ten three-illions, one meter in atomic nuclei diameters
Five-illions	16×10^{16}	One hundred sixty-five-illions, one mile in atomic nuclei diameters
Nine-illions	96×10^{28}	Nine hundred sixty-nine-illions, one light year in atomic nuclei diameters
Thirteen-illions	2×10^{40}	Twenty thirteen-illions, diameter of explored universe in atomic nuclei diameters

---

31 A marketing team at Marshall Fields Department Store in Chicago developed this word for Fuller in 1928, which they derived from iconic words he would use in describing his model for a low-cost mass-producible house he displayed there: "dynamic," "maximum," and "tension." Fuller continued to use this term during his life to identify his inventions.

we know of more than a billion such galaxies in thus-far-observed Universe.[32]

Any who think that humans on Earth are running Universe—or that Universe was created only to amuse or displease or bore humans—are obviously ignorant. Pay no attention to those who say, "Never mind that space stuff; let's get down to Earth; let's be realistic. We can't afford it." In reality we are so remote and infinitesimally tiny in space as to be almost nothing *but* space. The only reality is that of our sizeless minds, and the eternal metaphysical principles that they have discovered to be governing eternally regenerative Universe.

Since Earthians' astronomical measurements have only been conducted for a few thousand years, and nine-tenths of the information has been accumulated in the last five centuries, to be conservative, we can say that 11,000 years' exploration has brought in data covering 11 billion years. The ratio

$$\frac{11{,}000}{11 \text{ billion}} = \frac{1}{1 \text{ million}}$$

clearly manifests a high-order experiential acceleration in the rate of information gaining. Thus we take note of how really little we know and alert ourselves to the probability that the next decade will disclose what in effect must seem an entirely new Universe—so much more of the cosmically eternal a priori mystery will have been vouchsafed to us.

32 Current surveys, such as that by the Hubble Space Telescope in 1999, estimate the number of galaxies in the universe to be over one hundred billion. NASA, "Ask an Astrophysicist," http://imagine.gsfc.nasa.gov/docs/ask_astro/answers/021127a.html (accessed September 3, 2009).

Science and Humanities

Discoveries are uniquely regenerative to the explorer and are most powerful on those rare occasions when a generalized principle is discovered. When mind discovers a generalized principle permeating whole fields of special-case experiences, the discovered relationship is awesomely and elatingly beautiful to the discoverer personally, not only because to the best of his knowledge it has been heretofore unknown, but also because of the intuitively sensed potential of its effect upon knowledge and the consequent advantages accruing to humanity's survival and growth struggle in Universe. The stimulation is not that of the discoverer of a diamond, which is a physical entity that may be monopolized or exploited only to the owner's advantage. It is the realization that the newly discovered principle will provide spontaneous, common-sense logic engendering universal cooperation where, in many areas, only confusion and controversy had hitherto prevailed.

Whether it was my thick eyeglasses and lack of other personable favors, or because of some other psychological factors, I often found myself to be the number-one antifavorite amongst my schoolteachers and fellow students. When there were disturbances in the classroom, without looking up from his or her desk, the teacher would say, "One mark," or "Two marks," or "Three marks for Fuller." Each mark was a fifteen-minute penalty period to be served after the school had been let out for the

1975. Originally published by Fuller, in collaboration with E. J. Applewhite, in *Synergetics: Explorations in the Geometry of Thinking* (New York, 1975).

others. It was a sport amongst some of my classmates to arrange, through projectiles or other inventions, to have noises occur in my vicinity.

Where the teacher's opinion of me was unfavorable—and in the humanities this was, in the end, all that governed the marking of papers—I often found myself receiving lower grades for reasons irrelevant to the knowledge content of my work—such as my handwriting. But in science, and particularly in mathematics, the answers were either right or wrong. Probably to prove to myself that I might not be as low-average as was indicated by the gradings I got in the humanities, I excelled in my scientific classes and consistently attained the top grades because all my answers were correct. Maybe this made me like mathematics. My mathematics teachers in various years would say, "You seem to understand math so well, I'll show you some more if you stay in later in the afternoon."

I entered Harvard with all As in mathematics, biology, and the sciences, having learned in school advanced mathematics, which at that time was usually taught only at the college level. Since math was so easy for me, and finding it optional rather than compulsory at Harvard, I took no more of its courses. I was not interested in getting grades but in learning in areas that I didn't know anything about. For instance, in my freshman year I took not only the compulsory English A, but government, musical composition, art appreciation, German literature, and chemistry. However, I kept thinking all the time in mathematics and made progressive discoveries, ever enlarging my mathematical vistas. My elementary schoolwork in advanced mathematics as well as in physics and biology, along with my sense of security in relating those fields gave me great confidence that I was penetrating the unfamiliar while always employing the full gamut of rigorous formulation and treatment appropriate to testing the validity of intuitively glimpsed and tentatively assumed enlargement of the horizon of experientially demonstrable knowledge.

My spontaneous exploration of mathematics continued after I left Harvard. From 1915 to 1938 I assumed that what I had been discovering through the postcollege years was well known to mathematicians and other scientists, and was only the knowledge to which I would have been exposed had I stayed at Harvard and majored in those subjects. Why I did not continue at Harvard is irrelevant to academics. A subsequent special course at the U.S. Naval Academy, Annapolis, and two years of private tutelage by some of America's leading engineers of half a century ago completed my formally acknowledged "education."

In my twentieth year after college, I met Homer Lesourd, my old physics teacher, who most greatly inspired his students at my school, Milton Academy, and who for half a century taught mathematics at Harvard. We discovered to our mutual surprise that I had apparently progressed far afield from any of the known physio-mathematical concepts with which he was familiar. That was a third of a century ago. Thereafter, from time to time but with increasing frequency, I found myself able to elucidate my continuing explorations and discoveries to other scientists, some of whom were of great distinction. I would always ask them if they were familiar with any mathematical phenomena akin to the kind of disclosures I was making, or if work was being done by others that might lead to similar disclosures. I also asked them whether they thought my disclosures warranted my further pursuit of what was becoming an increasingly large body of elegantly integrated and coordinate field of omnirationally quantified vectorial geometry and topology. None of them could identify my discoveries with any of the scientific fields with which they were familiar, but they found no error in my disclosures and thought that the overall rational quantification and their logical order of unfoldment warranted my further pursuing the search.

When one makes discoveries that, to the best of one's knowledge and wide inquiry, seem to be utterly new, problems arise regarding the appropriate nomenclature and description of what is being discovered as well as problems of invention relating to symbolic economy and lucidity. As a consequence, I found myself inventing an increasingly large descriptive vocabulary, which evolved as the simplest, least ambiguous method of recounting the paraphernalia and strategies of all my relevant experiences.

For many years, my vocabulary was utterly foreign to the semantics of all the other sciences. I drew heavily on the dictionary for good and unambiguous terms to identify the multiplying nuances of my discoveries. In the meanwhile, the whole field of science was evolving rapidly in the new fields of quantum mechanics, electronics, and nuclear exploration, inducing a gradual evolution in scientific language. In recent years, I find my experiential mathematics vocabulary in a merging traffic pattern with the language trends of the other sciences, particularly physics.

Often, however, the particular new words chosen by others would identify phenomena other than that which I identify with the same words. As the others were unaware of my offbeat work, I had to determine for myself which of the phenomena had most logical claim to the names involved. I always conceded to other scientists, of course (unbeknownst to them), when they seemed to have prior or more valid claims. I would then invent or select appropriate but unused names for the phenomena I had discovered. But I held to my own claim when I found it to be eminently warranted or when the phenomena of other claimants were ill described by that term.

For example, quantum mechanics came many years after I did to employ the term *spin*. The physicists assured me that their use of the word did not involve any phenomena that truly spun. *Spin* was only a convenient word for describing certain unique energy behaviors and investments. My use of the term was to describe an experimentally demonstrable, inherent spinnability and unique magnitudes of rotation of an actually spinning phenomenon whose next fractional rotations were induced by the always co-occurring, generalized, a priori, environmental conditions within which the spinnable phenomenon occurred. I assumed that I held a better claim to the scientific term *spin*. In recent years spin has begun to be recognized by the physicists themselves as also inadvertently identifying a conceptually spinnable phenomenon—in fact, the same fundamental phenomenon I had identified much earlier by the word *spin*.

Because physics has found no continuums, no experimental solids, no things, no real matter, I had decided half a century ago to identify mathematical behaviors of energy phenomena only as *events*. If there are no things, there are no nouns of material substance. The old semantics permitted common-sense acceptance of such a sentence as "A man pounds the table," wherein a noun verbs a noun or a subject verbs a predicate. I found it necessary to change this form to a complex of events identified as *me,* which must be identified as a verb. The complex verb *me* observed another complex of events identified again ignorantly as a "table." I disciplined myself to communicate exclusively with *verbs*. There are no *wheres* and *whats;* only angle and frequency events described as *whens*.

In the competitive world of money making, discoveries are looked upon as exploitable and monopolizable claims to be operated as private properties of big business. As a consequence, the world has come to think of both discoveries and patents as monopolized property. This popular viewpoint developed during the last century, when both corporations and governments, supported by courts, have required individuals working for them to assign to them the patent rights on any discoveries or inventions made while in their employ. Employees were to assign these rights during, and for two years after termination of, their employment, whether the invention had been developed at home or at work.

The drafting of expert patent claims is an ever more specialized and complex art, involving expensive legal services usually beyond the reach of private individuals. When nations were remote from one another, internal country patents were effective protection. With today's omniproximities of the world's countries, only world-around patents costing hundreds of thousands of dollars are now effective, with the result that patent properties are available only to rich corporations.

So now most extant inventions belong to corporations and governments. However, invention and discovery are inherently individual functions of the minds of individual humans. Corporations are legal fabrications; they cannot invent and discover. Patents were originally conceived of as grants to inventors to help them recover the expenses of the long development of their discoveries, and they gave the inventor only a very short time to recover the expense. Because I am concerned with finding new technical ways of doing more with less, by which increasing numbers of humanity can emerge from abject poverty into states of physical advantage in respect to their environment, I have taken out many patent claims—first, to hold the credit of initiative for the inspiration received from humanity's needs and the theory of their best solution being that of the design revolution and not political revolution, and second, to try to recover the expense of development. But most importantly, I have taken the patents to avoid being stopped by others—in particular, corporations and governments—from doing what I felt needed doing.

But what often seems to the individual to be an invention, and seems also to be an invention to everyone he knows, time and again turns out to have been previously discovered when patent applications are filed and the search for prior patents begins. Sometimes dozens, sometimes hundreds, of patents will be found to have been issued, or applied for, covering the same idea. This simultaneity of inventing manifests a forward-rolling wave of logical exploration, the trends of which are generated by the omni-integrating discoveries and the subsequent inventions of new ways to employ the discoveries at an accelerating rate, which is continually changing the metaphysical environment of exploratory and inventive stimulation.

I have learned by experience that those who think only in competitive ways assume that I will be discouraged to find that others have already discovered, invented, and patented that which I had thought to be my own unique discovery or invention. They do not understand how pleased I am to learn that the task I had thought needed doing, and of which I had no knowledge of others doing, was happily already being well attended to, for my spontaneous commitment is to the advantage of all humanity. News of such work of others frees me to operate in other seemingly unattended but needed directions of effort. And I have learned how to find out more about what is or is not being attended to. This is evolution.

When I witness the inertias and fears of humans caused by technical breakthroughs in the realm of abstract scientific discovery, I realize that their criteria of apprehension are all uninformed. I see the same patterns of my experience amongst the millions of scientists around the world silently at work in the realm of scientific abstract discovery, often operating remote from one another. Many are bound to come out with simultaneous discoveries, each one of which is liable to make the others a little more comprehensible and usable.

Those who have paid-servant complexes worry about losing their jobs if their competitors' similar discoveries become known to their employers. But the work of pure science exploration is much less understood by the economically competitive-minded than is that of inventors. The great awards economic competitors give to the scientists make big news, but none of the great scientists ever did what they did in hope of earning rewards. The greats have ever been inspired by the a priori integrities of Universe and by the need of all humanity to move from the absolute ignorance of birth into a little greater understanding of the cosmic integrities. They esteem the esteem of those whom they esteem for similar commitment, but they don't work for it.

I recall now that when I first started making mathematical discoveries, years ago, my acquaintances would often say, "Didn't you know that Democritus made that discovery and said just what you are saying 2,000 years ago?" I replied that I was lucky that I didn't know that, because I thought Democritus so competent that I would have given up all my own efforts to understand the phenomena involved through my own faculties and investment of time. Rather than feeling dismayed, I was elated to discover that, operating on my own, I was able to come out with the same conclusion of so great a mind as that of Democritus. Such events increased my confidence in the resourcefulness and integrity of human thought purely pursued and based on personal experiences.

Mistake Mystique

"What do you think is the greatest challenge facing young people today as they prepare to assume their caretakership of this world?" was the question recently asked of me by a Midwestern high school student. From my viewpoint, by far the greatest challenge facing the young people today is that of responding and conforming only to their own most delicately insistent intuitive awarenesses of what the truth seems to them to be, as based on their own experiences and not on what others have interpreted to be the truth regarding events of which neither they nor others have experience-based knowledge.

This also means not yielding unthinkingly to "in" movements or to crowd psychology. This involves assessing thoughtfully one's own urges. It involves understanding, but not being swayed by, the spontaneous group spirit of youth. It involves thinking before acting in every instance. It involves eschewing all loyalties to other than the truth and love through which the cosmic integrity and absolute wisdom we identify inadequately by the name "God" speaks to each of us directly—and speaks only through our individual awareness of truth, and through our most spontaneous and powerful emotions of love and compassion.

The whole complex of omni-interaccommodative generalized principles thus far found by science to be governing all the behaviors of Universe altogether manifest an infallible wisdom's

April 1977. Originally published by Fuller in *East West Journal*.

interconsiderate, unified design, ergo an a priori, intellectual integrity conceptioning, as well as a human intellect discoverability. That is why youth's self-preparation for planetary caretakership involves commitment to comprehensive concern only with all humanity's welfaring; all the experimentally demonstrable, mathematically generalized principles thus far discovered by humans, and all the special case truths as we progressively discover them—the universally favorable synergetic consequences of which integrating commitments, unpredictable by any of those commitments when they are considered only separately—may well raise the curtain on a new and universally propitious era of humans in Universe.

By cosmic designing wisdom we are all born naked, helpless for months, and though superbly equipped cerebrally, utterly lacking in experience, ergo utterly ignorant. We were also endowed with hunger, thirst, curiosity, and procreative urge. We were designed predominantly of water—which freezes, boils, and evaporates within a minuscule temperature range. The brains' information apprehending, storing, and retrieving functions, as the control centers of the physical organisms employed by our metaphysical minds, were altogether designed to prosper initially only within those close thermal and other biospheric limits of planet Earth.

Under all the foregoing conditions, whatever humans have learned had to be learned as a consequence only of trial and error experience. Humans have learned only through mistakes. The billions of humans in history have had to make quadrillions of mistakes to have arrived at the state where we now have 150,000 common words to identify that many unique and only metaphysically comprehendible nuances of experience. The number of words in the dictionary will always multiply as we experience the progressive complex of cosmic episodes of Scenario Universe, making many new mistakes within the new set of unfamiliar circumstances. This provokes thoughtful reconsideration, and determination to avoid future mistake-making under these latest given circumstances. This in turn occasions the inventing of more incisively effective word tools to cope with the newly familiar phenomena.

Also by wisdom of the great design, humans have the capability to formulate and communicate from generation to generation their newly evolved thoughts regarding these lessons of greater experience which are only expressible through those new words, and thus progressively to accumulate new knowledge, new viewpoints, and new wisdom, by sharing the exclusively self-discovered significance of the new nuances of thought.

Those quadrillions of mistakes were the price paid by humanity for its surprising competence as presently accrued synergetically, for the first time in history, to cope successfully on behalf of all humanity with all problems of physically healthy survival, enlightening growth, and initiative accommodation.

Chagrin and mortification caused by their progressively self-discovered quadrillions of errors might long ago have given humanity such an inferiority complex that it would have become too discouraged to continue with the life experience. To avoid such a proclivity, humans were designedly given pride, vanity, and inventive memory, which altogether can and usually does tend to self-deception.

Witnessing the mistakes of others, the preconditioned crowd reflexing says, "Why did that individual make such a stupid mistake? We knew the answer all the time." So effective has been the nonthinking, group deceit of humanity that it now says, "Nobody should make mistakes," and punishes people for making mistakes. In love-generated fear for their children's future life in days beyond their own survival, parents train their children to avoid making mistakes lest they be put to social disadvantage.

Thus humanity has developed a comprehensive, mutual self-deception and has made the total mistake of not perceiving that realistic thinking accrues only after mistake-making which is the cosmic wisdom's most cogent way of teaching each of us how to carry on.

It is only at the moment of humans' realistic admission to themselves of having made a mistake that they are closest to that mysterious integrity governing Universe. Only then are humans able to free themselves of the misconceptions that have brought about their mistakes. With the misconceptions out of the way, they have their first view of the truth and, immediately, subsequent insights into the significance of the misconception as usually fostered by their pride and vanity, or by unthinking popular accord.

The courage to adhere to the truth as we learn it involves, then, the courage to face ourselves with the clear admission of all the mistakes we have made. Mistakes are sins only when not self-admitted. Etymologically, *sin* means *omission,* where *admission* should have occurred. An angle is a sinus, an opening, a break in a circle, an omission in the ever-evolving integrity of the whole human individual. Trigonometrically, the sine of an angle is the ratio of the length of the side facing the central angle considered, as ratioed to the length of the radius of the circle.

Human beings were given a left foot and a right foot to make a mistake first to the left, then to the right, left again and repeat. Between the over-controlled steering impulses, humans inadvertently attain the (between-the-two) desired direction of advance. This is not only the way humans work—it is the way Universe works. This is why physics has found no straight lines; it has found a physical Universe consisting only of waves.

Cybernetics, the Greek word for the steering of a boat, was first employed by Norbert Weiner to identify the human process of gaining and employing information. When a rudder of a ship of either the air or sea is angled to one side or the other of the ship's keel line, the ship's hull begins to rotate around its pivot point. The momentum of that pivoting tends to keep rotating the ship beyond the helmsman's intention. The helmsman therefore has to "meet" that course-altering momentum whose momentum in turn has again to be met. It is impossible to eliminate altogether the ship's course realterations. It is possible only to reduce the degree of successive angular errors by ever more sensitive, frequent, and gentle corrections. That's what good helmsmen or good airplane pilots do.

Norbert Weiner next invented the word *feedback* to identify discovery of all such biased errors and the mechanism of their over-corrections. In such angular error-correction systems (as governed, for instance, by the true north-holding direction sustained by the powerful angular momentum of gyroscopes which are connected by delicate hydro- or electrically actuated servomechanisms to the powerful rudder-steering motors), the magnitude of rightward and leftward veering is significantly reduced. Such automated steering is accomplished only by minimizing angular errors, and not by eliminating them, and certainly not by pretending they do not exist. Gyro-steering produces a wavi-linear course, with errors of much higher frequency of alternate correction and of much lesser wave depth than those made by the human handling of the rudder.

All designing of Universe is accomplished only through such alternating angle and frequency modulation. The DNA-RNA codes found within the protein shells of viruses which govern the designing of all known terrestrial species of biological organisms consist only of angle and frequency modulating instructions.

At present, teachers, professors, and their helpers go over the students' examinations, looking for errors. They usually ratio the percentage of error to the percentage of correctly remembered concepts to which the students have been exposed. I suggest that the teaching world alter this practice and adopt the requirement that all students periodically submit a written account of all the mistakes they have made, not only regarding the course subject, but in their self-discipline during the term, while also recording what they have learned from the recognition that they have made the mistakes; the reports should summarize what it is they have really learned, not only in their courses, but on their own intuition and initiative. I suggest, then, that the faculty be marked as well as the students on a basis of their effectiveness in helping the students to learn anything important about any subject—doing so by nature's prescribed trial and error leverage.

The more mistakes the students discover, the higher their grade. The greatest lesson that nature is now trying to teach humanity is that when the bumblebee goes after its honey, it inadvertently pollenizes the vegetation, which pollenization, accomplished at 90 degrees to the bumblebee's aimed activity, constitutes part of the link-up of the great ecological regeneration of the capability of terrestrial vegetation to impound upon our planet enough of the sun's radiation energy to support regeneration of life on our planet, possibly in turn to support the continuation of humans, whose minds are uniquely capable of discovering some of the eternal laws of Universe and thereby to serve as local Universe problem solvers in local maintenance of the integrity of eternal regeneration of Universe.

In the same indirect way, humanity is at present being taught by nature that its armament-making as a way to make a living for itself is inadvertently producing side effects of gained knowledge of how to do ever more with ever less and how, therewith, to render all the resources on Earth capable of successful support of all humanity. The big lesson, then, is called precession.[33] The 90-degree precessional resultants of the interaction of forces in Universe teach humanity that what it thought were the side effects are the main effects, and vice versa.

What, then, are the side effects of knowledge gained by students as a consequence of the teacher's attempt to focus the students' attention on single subjects? It can be that all the categories of informational educational systems' studies are like the honey-bearing flowers, and that the really important consequence of the educational system is not the special case information that the students

---

33 Fuller sees the principle of precession in a much broader context than most physics textbooks. He defines "precession" broadly as "the effect of bodies in motion on other bodies in motion."

gain from any special subject, but the side-effects learning of the interrelatedness of all things—and thereby the individual personal discovery of an overall sense of the omni-presence and reliability of generalized principles governing the omni-relatedness—whereby, in turn, the individuals discover their own cosmic significance as co-functions of the "otherness," which co-functioning is first responsible to all others (not self), and to the truth which is God, which embraces and permeates Scenario Universe.

The motto of Milton Academy, the Harvard preparatory school I attended, was "Dare to be True." In the crowd psychology and mores of that pre-World War I period, the students interpreted this motto as a challenge rather than an admonition, ergo, as "Dare to tell the truth as you see it and you'll find yourself in trouble. Better to learn how the story goes that everybody accepts and stick with that."

Ralph Waldo Emerson said, "Poetry means saying the most important things in the simplest way." I might have answered the initial student query in a much more poetical way by quoting only the motto of 340-year-old Harvard University, "Veritas"—Vere-i-tas—meaning progressively minimizing the magnitude of our veering to one side or the other of the star by which we steer whose pathway to us is delicately reflected on the sea of life and along whose twinkling stepping-stone path we attempt to travel toward that which is God—toward truth so exquisite as to be dimensionless, yet from moment to moment so reinformative as to guarantee the integrity of eternally regenerative Scenario Universe.

Veritas—it will never be superseded.

Children: The True Scientists

This book is for the only true scientists—the children.

The philosopher-scientist Sir James Jeans said: "Science is the attempt to set in order the facts of experience." The great Viennese physicist, Ernst Mach, whose name is used to identify ultrasonic airplane speeds—"Mach Number"—said, "Physics is the attempt to set the facts of experience in most economical order,"—the only raw material of all science is experience.

Children are born true scientists. They spontaneously experiment and experience and reexperience again. They select, combine, and test, seeking to find order in their experiences—"Which is the mostest? Which is the leastest?" They smell, taste, bite, and touch-test for hardness, softness, springiness, roughness, smoothness, coldness, warmness; they heft, shake, punch, squeeze, push, crush, rub, and try to pull things apart. True scientists deal only in the experienceable and base their assumptions only upon the physically re-demonstrable behaviors and characteristics.

Innocently betrayed by the equally innocently detoured-from-reality educational system, the young scientists are lured into forsaking their innate true-scientist advantage by adopting the school-taught mathematical tools with which to probe, sort out, and reassociate their experience-won information, most of which mathematical tools are experimentally nondemonstrable assumptions. In the school-taught mathematics, reality is "three-dimensional."

1977. Originally published as an introduction to Einar Thorsteinn, *Nature's Forms (Barnaleikur)* (Reykjavik, 1977).

Can you demonstrate physically a real something having no weight, no temperature, no longevity? Try to demonstrate a structural model of the subdimensional "point" of which the schoolteachers and professional mathematicians pretend to themselves that their one-dimensional lines, their two-dimensional planes, and their three-dimensional realities are constructed. To give simple proof of nice, simple plane geometry you must demonstrate physically the "surface" of nothing. Try to produce a structural model of the square root of minus one or a structural model of eternally unfinishable π (pi).

The Massachusetts Institute of Technology's Department of Mathematics catalog states "Mathematics is the science of structure and pattern in general." Humanity's invention and adoption of the word *image* and its brain-formed employment as *image-ination* was occasioned by the need to describe to others the visual experiencing of structural conceptions—images. "Seeing" always and only occurs inside the brain. "Seeing" always occurs only as brain constructs—*image*-ination. Professional scientists deceive themselves by adopting such nonexperienceable "tools" as unimaginable *imaginary numbers.*

Victims of their nondemonstrable, ergo self-deluding, mathematical assumptions (axioms), academic scientists have been forced to improvise a vast complex of speculative techniques for coping three-dimensionally with an inherently four- and more-dimensional reality. They have been forced as well to adopt a plurality of incommensurable fraction constants with which to compensate for their use of a mathematical coordinate system other than that employed by physical Universe. Nonunitarily conceptual, eternally self-regenerative, Scenario Universe's "here" differentiating, and "there" integrating complex of nonsimultaneous and only partially overlapping energy intertransforming episodes, and their interdependent effects complementations, always and only operate as (a) angularly convergent, gravitationally importive, syntropic, substantive, structural-systems' concentratings, and

(b) angularly divergent, radiantly exportive, entropic, destructural dispersings, and never in the always and only immutable frame of behavioral data reference of conventional education's and academic science's three only omni-interperpendicularly, self-interacting sets of always only interparalleled, eternally extensive, absolutely straight lines, which straight lines are 180-degree angles. Nature uses only waves—never straight lines.

All mathematicians assume that a plurality of lines can passage through the same dimensional point at the same time, whereas physicists find that a physical-reality line is an energy event and that only one energy event can transit a given locus at a given time, all of which accounts for the physical interference patterns and angular reflections, refractions, and smash-up dispersions visibly occurring in their particle bombardment cloud chambers. Academic science has found no solids in nature, yet conceptually confused physics identifies one of its most advanced activities as "solid-state" physics. Arduously employing the formulae of calculus's cofunctioning and infinitesimally deviating fluctions from their originally perpendicular-parallel "x-y-z" line of reference, professional scientists sometimes arrive at quantations having reasonable agreement with the quantities demonstrated by physical experiment. Having learned awkwardly, circuitously, and fortuitously to cope, they hold grimly to their educational formulae. Their invisible cobweb-weaving in the dark being the only scientific method of which they know and with which they have become painstakingly familiar, academic scientists hold meticulously to it and therefore succeed in indoctrinating less than one-tenth of 1 percent of humanity to a degree of professional cleverness adequate to cope meaningfully with experimentally developed data in the frontiers of scientific advance.

This innocently acquired dilemma of humanity is now correctable because persistent childlike integrity of exploration, employing only experimentally evidenceable tools and strategies, has discovered and demonstrated the omnirational mathematical coordinate system being employed by eternally regenerative Scenario Universe. Its discoverer has named it "synergetics."[34] If it becomes popularly adopted, synergetics has been discovered just in time to avert comprehensive disaster for all humanity. In many religious scriptures it is prophesied that if and when humanity attains salvation, "a little child shall lead them." This could be modified to read, "the only true scientists, the children, shall lead humanity's way with their experimentally demonstrable, omnirational coordinate mathematics." How and why may this occur?

Within the realm of design science and engineering, it is now incontrovertibly demonstrable that if humanity employs the sum of its knowledge and pools all the world's resources, we now have aboard our Spaceship Earth more than ample capability to take care of all humanity for all generations to come and to do so at higher standards of living and individual freedom than any humans have thus far experienced or even dreamed of, while in no way endangering the ecological integrity of our planet. This is to say that we have 4 billion billionaires aboard our planet whom the competitive expediencies of our present [1977] cultural economic system are inadvertently depriving of realizing their good fortune.

It is also incontrovertibly demonstrable that it is feasible to accomplish this lasting success for all humans within ten years while concurrently phasing out all further human use of fossil fuels and atomic energy. We can live handsomely on our annual energy income from the sun and the many modes of its impoundment by our planet's biospheric and ecological energy intertransformings.

Why aren't we spontaneously doing this? First, because humanity has for all time past been convinced that there is a lethal inadequacy of life support on our planet. This misconception

---

34 Fuller, referring to himself here, published *Synergetics: Explorations in the Geometry of Thinking* in 1975, reviewing his life-long geometrical discoveries—it is 676 pages long. In 1979, he published a second volume, *Synergetics 2*, which is 592 pages. While currently out of print, an online edition, which integrates volumes 1 and 2 as Fuller wished it would ultimately be published, can be found at http://www.synergetics.info.

engendered political and religious organizations, all of which pro-claim that they can lead their devout followers to special salva-tion. Each political system says, "You may or may not like our system, but we are convinced that it is the fairest, most logical and ingenious system for coping with lethal inadequacy of life support, wherefore you have the best chance of surviving if you join our group; but because there are others who disagree and think they have the only adequate system, it can only be resolved by trial of arms which is fittest to survive." Thus technology is employed exclusively on a partisan basis.

We now have 150 sovereign-state admirals simultaneously in command of our one and only Spaceship Earth. We have the star-board side of the ship trying to sink the port side, and the stern try-ing to secede from the rest of the ship. All the political and religious systems have demonstrated only increasing incapability to cope effectively on behalf of their side, let alone for all humanity.

Only a new kind of revolution can solve the problems. Unlike history's past politically and religiously commanded revolutions, realizing the now-feasible, physical success for all humanity in-volves an applied-science revolution whose total success for all will forever invalidate any and all of the one-sided rationalizing ramifications of selfishness and exclusivity. Attainment of physical success for all cannot be accomplished by political strategy. It can-not be accomplished by private enterprise's unilateral advantage seeking. It cannot be accomplished by priestly intercession. It can only be accomplished by a design revolution which produces so much higher technical performance per each unit of resource in-vested as to take care of all human needs. It can be accomplished, only through each of the individuals of all humanity first acquir-ing experimental knowledge of the child-discovered, completely lucid, mathematical coordinate system employed by nature, and thereby in turn spontaneously comprehending structure, lever-age, and mechanical advantage, and thereby in turn learning that it is technically feasible to attain lasting physical success for all humanity, and thereafter setting about spontaneously to accomplish that success; second, by humanity-at-large's apprehending that this can be accomplished only if it is for all humanity; and third, by humanity-at-large's recognizing that the accomplishment of lasting physical success for all also requires development of universal scientific and technical comprehension and physically demonstrable technological competence.

Because people know how to use a telephone, to drive a car, and to travel by airplane does not mean that they understand science and technology. At present there are 40 million scientists and engineers on planet Earth—that is only 1 percent of humanity. Ninety-nine percent of humanity does not understand science and technology because, of the innate scientists (grown children), 99 percent do not understand the physically nondemonstrable mathematical language of science. Not understanding science and technology, the 99 percent do not know that all that science has discovered, and continues to discover, is that physical Universe is naught but a complex of technology—the most elegantly efficient, effective, and interconsiderate technology. Not understanding that the blue sky, clouds, birds, mountains, trees, and great seas, as well as the ecology that regenerates them, are all of the most exquisite technological design so superb as to be observationally different from humanity's thus-far developed, crudely gross, technological designings. The prime difference between humanity's thus-far developed technology and that of nature's biological designing is that nature solves her compression problems by load distributing hydraulics, and humans solve compression problems only by nonload-distributing "solid" crystalline substances.

Because 99 percent of humanity does not understand what science has learned, that 99 percent equates technology only with its partisan uses as weaponry and money-making machinery. This dilemma of humanity's technological ignorance can be cured only by education of the 99 percent to the fact that nature herself is not using the nondemonstrable mathematical coordinate system of science, but instead is using a lucidly demonstrable system, with which natural and comprehendible system the majority of humanity can quickly discover for itself that its omnisuccessful continuance on this planet can be attained only through a technological design-science revolution.

Fortunately, we can now report that an educational revolution is occurring—one in which only synergetics' experimentally demonstrable geometry is employed. It is based on the discovery of the relative energy investment values of nature's geometrical hierarchy of cosmically primitive structurings and intertransformings. It is the geometry of general systems. All of its lines are vectors—that is, they exist only as energetic phenomena. A vector always represents the product of mass, multiplied by the velocity of a given energy entity operating in a given angular direction in respect to a given axis of observational reference. Synergetics discloses by physical models the orderly ways in which nature intertransforms, propagates, pulsates, sometimes visibly and sometimes invisibly, yet is always demonstrably operative by "tuning in" and "tuning out."

Einar Thorsteinn has written and illustrated this book and has developed extremely simple drawings which make synergetics conceptually inspiring and informative—to both children and grown people. He designed beautifully cut-out drawings with which anyone can produce the family of primitive structures to become familiar with both the symmetry, the relative numerical volume values, and the topological characteristics of nature's hierarchy of primitive structurings.

Making these beautiful synergetic models and placing them on display in homes and schools will swiftly accommodate young humanity's self-education in the fundamentals of scientific exploration and development. This will be one of the fortunate events leading to the general comprehension and spontaneously demonstrated competence essential to sustain human survival on this planet.

Where Will the World Be in 2025?

You ask, "Where will the world be in 2025?" Sometimes people use the word world to mean the whole universe, "the most beautiful girl in all the world," sometimes much more limitedly as "in the sports world" but I take it that you mean the *planet Earth* together with all the human beings gravitationally cohered to it around its 200 million square miles of surface. If that is your definition of the world, then I reply, "The world will as yet be orbiting around the sun as the sun and its planets merry-go-round with the galactic system." Whether the unique chemical constituents of humans will as yet be anthropomorphically organized and as yet healthily serving the weightless mysterious phenomenon life on board Spaceship Earth is the touch-and-go, yes-and-no question. Whether or not humans will be alive on our planet will, however, probably be resolved by cosmic evolution as early as 1985. We don't have to wait until 2025 to find out. Human beings, unlike any other known phenomena, have been given minds with which to discover abstract, weightless principles operating in Universe, and employ those principles in apprehending and treating discretely with the exclusively mathematical information regarding celestial chemistry and physics occurring in stars tens of billions of light years away from the little planet Earth. In contradistinction to the human *mind's* unique capability of discovering generalized and only mathematically stateable, complexedly covarying interrelationships existing between

April 1975. Originally published in the *Philadelphia Daily News*.

and not in any of the geometrical, chemical, or physical characteristics of any of the separate parts of complex systems, human *brains*
as well as the brains of other creatures deal only with the unique
sensorial inputs of each special case experience; the special color,
sound, size, touch, feel, and smell of that particular experience.
Minds deal in eternal transsensorially apprehendable, covariant,
interrelationship principles. We humans were given this capability
to function as local Universe problem solvers. We are here to solve
evolutionarily occurring, unprecedented, metaphysical, as well as
physical, problems. We can do so by means of our unique access
to the thus-far discovered inventory of eternal principles.

Universe is eternally regenerative. Universe is everywhere continually intertransforming in accordance with the abstract, weightless principles of which (so far as we know) only the human mind
has cognizance.

As of the closing of 1974, muscle and power are in complete
dominance over world affairs. The world pays two pugilists $3
million to pummel one anothers' brain boxes for a dozen minutes
in front of the TV cameras. The winner is officially adulated by
the United States Congress. He's a good human being so that's
great but no TV shows are celebrating far greater metaphysical
battle heroes and heroines in their silent commitment to love and
truth, who every day sacrifice themselves for others. For the last
two decades the world powers have been spending $200 billion
annually for armaments and only negligible amounts to assuage
poverty.[35] The most powerfully armed control the world's wealth.
Power and muscle clearly continue in the world's saddle.

Whether human beings will be on our planet in the twenty-first
century depends on whether mind has reversed this condition and
has come into complete control over muscle and physical power
in general; as a consequence of which, the world will at last be
operational by humans for all humans.

---

35 See note 19, p. 139.

Humans will be alive aboard our planet Earth in the twenty-first century only if the struggle for existence has been completely disposed of by providing abundant life support and accommodation for all humans. Only under these conditions can all humans function as competent local Universe problem solvers. That is what humans were invented for. Only if Abraham Lincoln's "right" has come into complete ascendancy over "might" will humanity remain alive on board our planet in the twenty-first century, and if so, it will be here for untold millenniums to come. Humanity is now going through its final examination as to whether it can qualify for its Universe function and thereby qualify for continuance on board the planet.

It is not necessary to pick the half-century-away year 2025 to permit enough changes to develop to warrant journalistic reporting of prognostications. It is a matter of human beings getting into the twenty-first century at all. If we do make it, the acceleration in the rate of occurrence of unprecedented, utterly unpredicted, incredibly great technological, economic, and social changes will be almost (but not necessarily) devastating. Human beings are not aboard our minuscule planet just to be pleased or displeased. Humanity's mind-evolved-technology has now photographed a billion galaxies, each of 100 billion stars, surrounding minuscule Earth to an observed radius of 11 billion light years, 99.9 percent of which are invisible to the naked eye. Before the close of the twentieth century humans may well be transceiver-transmitted from here to there by radio and will be traveling back and forth between the base spaceship, Earth, and various local Universe problem centers. Transceived by radio will mean traveling at 700 million miles per hour to attend to humanity's local cosmic problem solving functions.

If humans pass their cosmic exam as local Universe problem solvers and continue on the planet into the twenty-first century, there will be no thoughts whatsoever of *earning a living*. There will be no thoughts of, or even such words as, *business competition, money,* or *lies,* for such phenomena will be historically extinct. Such words as *politics, war, weapons, debt* will be only of historical significance.

Electronic means will have been highly developed for continually inventorying of all of humanity's thoughts, volitions, and dispositions regarding all currently evolving problems. Humanity will know at all times what the unique majority volitions may be regarding each and every currently recognized and considered problem.

There will be one world management organization similar to but greatly improved over those of the twentieth century United States "city-manager" functions. The one world management will be taking its instructions directly from the computer readout volitions of the majority. When the majority discovers a given decision is leading humanity into trouble, the popular realization will be immediately computer manifest and the world management will alter the course accordingly. This feed-back servo mechanism is the same as that employed in "automatic" flight controls and in the steering of ships. The popular view will be immediately served by the management with no searching for scapegoats when erroneous decisions are discovered and corrected.

All human beings engaged in common wealth production or research and development will be doing so entirely on their own volition because that is what they will want to be doing. They will have to qualify for their membership on any production team as they now qualify for participation in Olympic games. That which is plentiful will be socialized. That which is scarce must be used only for total advantage and must be used only in the research instruments and tools-that-make-tools which produce the plentiful end products for humanity.

All of humanity will be enjoying not only all of Earth but a great deal of local Universe. "Where do you live?" "I live on the moon," or "I live on Spaceship Earth," will be the kinds of answers.

Some large number of human beings will be engaged in archeological research, as humanity will want to know a great deal more about the historical occupancy of our planet by humans. The important original buildings of antiquity will be rebuilt or restored as Babylon is now being rebuilt, and artifacts from world-around museums will be returned to original sites and reintroduced to function as of yore. Thus research teams can live experimentally at various historical control periods of history thus to elucidate much of the wisdom gained in the past.

While everybody will know much of what everybody is thinking, individuality will not cease but will increase. What people are thinking spontaneously as a consequence of the interaction of the unique patterns of their inherited genes and their own experiences will make personalities even more interesting one to the other. Intuition will be fostered. Communication will probably be accomplished by thinking alone, ergo more swiftly and more realistically than by sound and words.

Omniconsiderate, comprehensive, synergetic integrity will be the aesthetic criteria, and its humanly evolved designs will come to do so much with so very little as to attain the ephemeral beauty heretofore manifest only by nature in its formulation of flowers, crystals, stars, and the pure love of a child.

Whether humanity will pass its final exams for such a future is dependent on you and me, not on somebody we elect or who elects themselves to represent us. We will have to make each decision both tiny and great with critical self-examination—"Is this truly for the many or just for me?" If the latter prevails it will soon be "curtains" for all.

We are in for the greatest revolution in history. If it's to pull the top down and it's bloody, all lose. If it is a design-science revolution to elevate the bottom and all others as well to unprecedented new heights, all will live to dare spontaneously to speak and live and love the truth, strange though it often may seem.

Learning Tomorrows
Education for a Changing World

I'm deeply convinced that the subject of Learning Tomorrows contains within it the answer as to whether humanity is going to be able to continue much longer on our planet—for we are going to have to acquire an almost entirely new educational system and do so almost "overnight." We are going to have to learn why humans have been included in the design of eternally regenerative Universe and thereafter swiftly to start fulfilling that cosmic function. I therefore feel an enormous responsibility being allowed to be on your platform to discuss such a subject.

The first thing I think about is Professor Percival Bridgman of Harvard, the natural philosopher who, at the turn of the nineteenth into the twentieth century said, "How do you suppose it happened that Einstein surprised all the scientists? Why were all the scientists caught off-guard?" Bridgman looked deeply into this matter and concluded that the reason that Einstein caught all the scientists off-guard was that Einstein was what Bridgman called "operational"; that is, he paid complete attention to, and interconsidered all the circumstances surrounding any scientific discovery. He did not isolate the discovery, but paid attention to all the circumstances of its occurrence.

I'm going to suggest a way of thinking about Einstein and his operational way of looking at things. This is not an example that

1979. First published in *Learning Tomorrows: Commentaries on the Future of Education*, ed. Peter H. Wagschal (New York, 1979).

he—Einstein—himself used, but it is my own and has become popularly adopted.

We have a man riding across the country, going due west, on a railroad train. He leans out the window and drops a flaming apple. He has another scientist with him, and the other scientist has a sextant to measure angles and he has stopwatches. They make observations of the flaming apple's trajectory, which they see flying backwards—that is, to the east, and they measure the angular distances it seems to travel and how much time at each angle. There are two other scientists standing to the north of the railroad at the time the foregoing event occurs. They have sextants, compasses, and stopwatches. They see the apple come out the window traveling *westward,* and gradually descending to the track. Using their sextants and stopwatches they make accurate observations of exactly what they see. We have another scientist who is standing on the railroad track far to the west, and she sees the flaming apple go very slowly down toward the earth. We have another person who is standing under the railway trestle when this all occurs, and she makes her scientifically recorded observation. We find that all these observations were faithfully made, and yet they were all different. They tallied what distances and in what directions the various observers were from the flaming object, and how much of an angle it moved through, and at what rate. So this brought Einstein into thinking about such variable situations and reports as being *relative,* not only to one another, but also to all other known cosmic variables. Einstein would observe that the rotation of Earth affected the event. Earth, the train, the observers and the flaming apple were all also zooming around the sun at 60,000 miles per hour.

It is very important to realize that Einstein not only was a teacher but was also an examiner in the Swiss Patent Office, reviewing patents. At this time, the most prominent products of Switzerland were clocks and watches. If you were reading patent claims of people inventing time-keeping devices, the first thing you would discover is that none of the devices are accurate. They all come out of production differently. In each, the producer tries to provide a little more accuracy. I'm sure this made Einstein think very much about Isaac Newton's assumption of time as being a phenomenon that permeated all Universe uniformly and simultaneously. Newton's was an instant, omni-everywhere *exact* Universe. This brought Einstein into thinking about *relative accuracies* and so forth.

I want to give you an example of non-operational procedures in our own schoolroom experience: the teacher goes to the blackboard and says, "You're going to have your first geometry lesson." And the teacher draws a square, and tells you that a square is an area bound by a closed line consisting of four equal-length edges and four right angles. All the successive plane geometrical figures are accomplished as areas within "closed lines." While drawing, the teacher says, "A triangle is an area *bound* by a closed line of three edges and three angles."

In all these plane geometry figures, we are taught to see only the little figures that are drawn on the board. We look only at the area bound by the closed line. We tend to think about only the geometry on the inside of the line. On the outer side of the line, the teacher is asking you to assume that the blackboard surface extends outward to infinity. Therefore the outer area is, to the teacher, "undefinable."

But the operational fact is that the blackboard *doesn't* go to infinity; it gets to its four edges and goes around to the back. It is a finite object. It is a board. It has length and breadth and thickness. The teacher drew on the surface of a closed system. When the teacher drew a triangle, the total surface of the blackboard was divided into two areas by the closed line. The teacher made two triangles. There is the little one to which the teacher pointed, but all the rest of the blackboard is an area bound by a closed line, having also three edges and three angles. Unscrew your blackboard from the wall. Make your little triangle and then check the remainder of the blackboard's surface, front, edges, and back, and you will find the other complementary big triangle. The fact that it goes around to the back does not alter the fact that it is a continuous surface area bound by a closed line of three angles. We were not taught to look at things that way. The board's edges, when viewed through a lens, are rounded, continuous surfaces. Edges are not terminal conditions. They are short radius turnabout conditions. Möbius's strip has an "inside" of the paper and "outside" of the paper. It is a flattened substance but it *does not* have two sides divided by its "edge lines."

I say to a young man, "Draw me a triangle on the ground." And he draws it, and I say, "You've drawn *four* triangles." And he says, "No, I've drawn only one." I have to show him that he has drawn four triangles. A triangle is an area bound by a closed line with three edges and three angles. You'll agree with me that you've drawn it on Earth. I'm going to take an Earth "globe" and make a closed line of it, which we call the equator. It is a circle—a closed line, and it divides the whole Earth into two areas—a southern hemisphere and a northern hemisphere. Let's go all the way to the North Pole, draw a circle around your feet. It divides the total surface of Earth into two areas—a large southern and a very small but very real northern—real because we are standing on it. Now let's draw a triangle around our feet instead of a circle. Now we've divided Earth's whole surface into two areas, both of them bound by a closed line with three edges and three angles. And the student said, "You must be wrong. The three corners have outside angles of 300 degrees each for a total of 900 degrees. The sum of the angles of a triangle is always 180 degrees." I said, "Where did you hear that?" He said, "Well, they taught me that in school." I said, "The school is wrong. The angles of a triangle never add to 180 degrees. I've got to prove that to you also."

We have what is called a "great circle." A great circle is a line formed on the surface of a sphere by a plane which goes through the center of the sphere. A great circle is the shortest distance between two points on the surface of a sphere. I'm going also to have to prove that to you. I pick up a twelve-inch Earth globe, saying, "I'm going to pick a latitude circle, which is what we call a lesser circle, because it doesn't go through the center of the sphere. I point to the latitude circle of 80-degrees north latitude. I take a pair of dividers—and put one end of the divider on the North Pole and the other end on the lesser circle of 80-degrees north latitude Figure 7. With the dividers fixed at that 10-degree radius opening, I now put one end of the divider on the equator and strike a circle exactly the same size as that of the 80-degree north latitude circle. You now see the equator with the little 80-degree north latitude circle superimposed. With its center on the equator, the little circle crosses the equator at two points—A and B. Quite clearly it is a shorter distance between A and B on the equator than it is on the little circle. I just want to convince you that great circles are always the shortest surface distances between points on a sphere. In spherical trigonometry, we always use great-circle arcs for the "lines" connecting points on a sphere.

I'm going to look again at our Earth globe. Starting at the North Pole, I take a meridian of longitude, which is a great circle, and go from the North Pole down to the equator Figure 8. The meridian impinges on the equator at 90 degrees because the equator is produced by a spinning of Earth around the north-south axis through which the great-circle plane of the meridian runs. So, I leave the meridian, turn 90 degrees, and walk eastwardly on the equator. I changed my course 90 degrees. I now go one-quarter of the way around Earth at the equator, and take a meridian northward, leaving the equator at 90 degrees. I go back to the North Pole. Because I went one-quarter way around Earth on the equator, the angle of my return to the North Pole is 90 degrees from my starting meridian, so we've got three corners, each of 90 degrees—90-90-90—for a total of 270 degrees, not 180 degrees, as the sum of the angles of a very real triangle, on the surface of Earth.

Figure 7

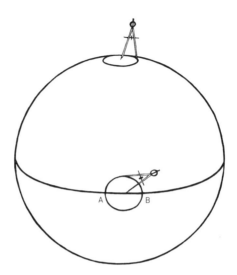

Figure 8

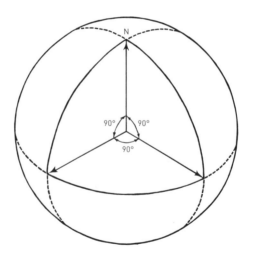

Now, see figure 3 ^{Figure 9}. We're going to bisect the edges of that 90-90-90-degree triangle, and interconnect the midpoints with great-circle arcs to produce a smaller great-circle triangle whose corners are 70.5288 degrees each. Bisect that smaller triangle's three great-circle arc-edges. Interconnect those midpoints with great-circle arc-lines and get an even smaller triangle, and the three corner angles are 62.9643 degrees each. Bisect that smallest triangle's three arc-edges. Interconnect the midpoints and get an even smaller triangle with corner angles of 60.7664 degrees. Bisect its arc-edges, interconnect the midpoints and get corner angles of 60.1933 degrees. With each smaller triangle, each corner approaches 60 degrees but never gets to 60; that is, the sum of the angles of an approximately flat triangle is approximately +180 degrees, a limit case which is never reached. The sum of the three angles of all physical triangles always adds up to something other than 180 degrees.

Incidentally, you and I were taught about fractions in school. We were taught how to multiply and divide them, and so forth; we were taught, also, that we couldn't have peanuts divided by elephants. You had to be dealing entirely with peanuts or entirely with elephants. So, when later on we took trigonometry, we were upset when we came to the trigonometric functions, called sines and cosines, tangents and cotangents, and other unfamiliar new words. "What is a function?" I asked. The teacher said, "Draw a picture of a right-angled triangle. It has six parts—angles A, B, and C, and three lines, a, b, and c ^{Figure 10}. The corner angle C is known because it is a right angle (90 degrees). The trigonometric functions are ratios between any two of the five unknown parts of that right triangle. This means we have ratios between an angle and a line. Ratios are expressed mathematically as fractions. This means we have fractions in which we divide *lines* by angles or angles by lines." But I had learned that I can't make a fraction out of peanuts and elephants, how can I have fractions of lines divided by angles?

Figure 9

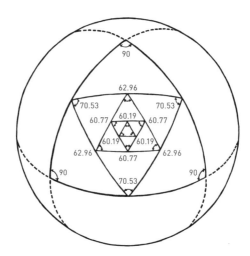

Figure 10

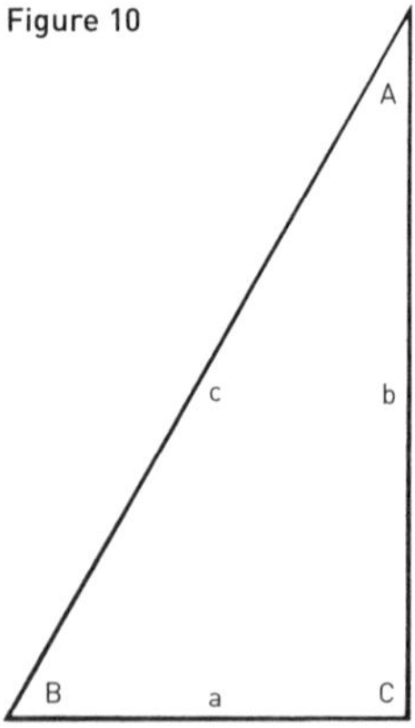

Figure 11

In order to answer that question, I need to be able to make a drawing on a symmetrical something. A simple way is to draw on a sphere. So let's make a triangle on the surface of an apple, drawn with a knife. With the point of the knife, I draw a great-circle-edged triangle on the apple's surface. Then, using the knife's blade, I cut inwardly on each of the edge lines of the triangle—to the apple's center ^{Figure 11}, and see that what we call the "edges" or arcs of the triangle are in *operational fact* the "central angles." We are dividing surface angles by central angles, which is absolutely valid. We are not dividing angles by lines after all.

The fact is that we think spontaneously about omnidimensional reality, but were taught at school that real life is much too complicated, so they give you their "nice, simple, plane geometry."

They tell you they are starting you with a two-dimensional plane.

Now, I'd like somebody to give me experimental evidence of a surface of *nothing*. That's where we made the first great operational mistake with that blackboard, by saying it had a surface of nothing—and that the plane went laterally to infinity. There is no infinity. No scientist has ever been there to give demonstrable evidence.

What we should realize is that we're always dealing experientially with something, and all somethings have both insides and outsides. You learn only in reality by starting off with experience-able somethings. If you really are drawing on *something,* all your lines are measures of central angles.

This is what Bridgman was getting at about Einstein. What are the real physical world circumstances? Don't assume false circumstances where the real circumstances can be found.

The boy to whom I am showing these experiences now agrees with me that, inadvertently, he was wrong about the big triangle as well as the little triangle. He says, "But I didn't mean to make the big triangle," and I say that that is the trouble with what humanity is doing today. We've been taught to look at only one side of closed lines. We have a bias—*my* family, *my* house, *my* country.

But everything we do is always going to affect not only us, but also all the rest of planet Earth and Universe. The very littlest things we do on Earth always greatly affect total Universe.

Then my student says, "You said I had drawn four triangles. You have now proved to me that I've drawn two—a very big one and a very little one, but where are the other two?" I said, "Well, you can only draw on something, and that something always has an inside and an outside." Any something—we'll call all somethings "systems"—divides all Universe into four parts: (1) all Universe outside the system, (2) all Universe inside the system; and a little bit of Universe which is the system that does the dividing, which itself subdivides into two parts, i.e., (3) and (4); one the outward "convex" (3), and the inward "concave" (4). Convex and concave always and only coexist.

When energy as radiation impinges on concave, the latter concentrates the radiation into a beam. When radiation impinges on a convex surface, the radiation is diffused. So convex and concave have completely different physical effects, yet they always and only coexist. I say to the boy, "What you've done is not only to draw the big surface and little surface triangles, but you've divided the whole Universe into an insideness and an outsideness. You made, then, a big concave triangle and a little concave triangle, and you made a big convex triangle and a little convex triangle. You made four triangles. You can never make a real Universe triangle without making four. This is the way everything begins with fourness." This is the four-dimensional world in which we live.

All that I have been explaining is what Professor Percival Bridgman meant by "operational." There was much abstract philosophical discussion about "reality" at Harvard, led by Peirce,[36] just before the turn of the nineteenth into the twentieth century, which Peirce called the "school of pragmatism." In contradistinction to Peirce's abstract epistemology, Bridgman wanted a title for

---

36 Charles Sanders Peirce (1839–1914), American philosopher and founder of "pragmatism."

a scientific grand strategy that is more than pragmatic, and he used the word *operational*. This meant dealing comprehensively and incisively with scientifically re-demonstrable reality and in strictly scientific quantation. The word *operational* has become very much used and misused since that time.

What I've been telling you about, really, is operational mathematics. There is always an experiential reality. There is no way you can abstract yourself and take a position outside Universe. You are always in Universe. As integral functions of Universe, whatever we do affects the whole Universe, every time. We are all complementary parts of Universe.

I have one rubber glove, a red rubber glove, and I have it on my left hand, it fits on my left hand beautifully. I'm going to start stripping it off my left hand by rolling the bottom of the cuff of it. As I do, I find it's green on the inside. I keep roll-pulling it, and finally it comes off, and now the red left hand has been annihilated, we have only a right hand and it is green. What we do locally is complementary to the rest of Universe. There's the rest of Universe that fits around my hand, around my body, that is also altered by any, every act. It's always there—that ever, everywhere intertransforming, nonsimultaneously episoded, eternally regenerative Universe.

To comprehend more clearly, we have to electromagnetize our thinking and our communicative vocabulary. What we tune in and what we don't tune in doesn't make the nontuned-in nonexistent. This electromagnetic cerebrating seems to induce a very different way of thinking about things, than about static space and solid things—some*things* and no*things*. We're always dealing with thinkable systems which are only subdivisions of nonunitarily conceptual Scenario Universe. A system is a tuned-in episode and not a thing.

I'm confident that the way I am talking to you is part of Education for Tomorrow. Operational comprehensivity and detail are going to spell the difference between whether the world fails to understand what its potentials and realizable options are, and whether we comprehend enough about the function of humans in Universe to be able to employ our mind and exercise our options to establish lasting physical success for all—or perish. We are going to have to learn that it is going to have to be success for all humanity or for none; that goes for an even larger way of thinking which says it is going to have to be total cosmic success which includes humanity, or it is going to be cosmic quits.

We must get over the idea of trying to oversimplify education and make it "simple" by making it unreal, isolated, nonoperational. I became convinced as time went on that it is easy to consider myself always as a function of Universe and to remove false premises and to learn that everything I have ever *really* learned has come from seeing myself in the context of the cosmic working premise. This is the context in which I have been speaking to you.

The next thing I would like to talk about is human beings in Universe right now: how and why we are here. Let us try to understand what all our local problems are, and what all problems everywhere are, and what problems have to do with human beings in Universe.

I think that because you and I are so tiny, and our Earth is so big, and Universe is so incredibly incomprehensible—we're not thinking very realistically about the rest of that Universe.

When I was twenty-eight years of age, Hubble first discovered another galaxy. In the fifty-five years since that time, we have found a billion such galaxies.[37] We are surrounded by an incredible amount of information which was not available when I was young, and I want you to think very rapidly with me about our circumstances and our scale. Our planet Earth is 8,000 miles in diameter. Our highest mountains are approximately 5 miles above sea level, and our oceans' deepest points, about 5 miles below sea level, so there is a 10-mile differential between the innermost and

---

37 See note 32, p. 152.

outermost surface points on our planet Earth. Ten miles in relation to 8,000 miles is only 1/800. If I take a twelve-inch polished steel ball and breathe on it, the depth of my condensed breathing upon it (1/100 inch) is deeper than the ocean on our planet.

I want to think of us on our real planet Earth. We have *photographs* of our Earth taken from space, and you can see the blue of the water and the brown of the land, but you can't make out mountains, or see the depth of the oceans. You can't see any such differential.

Humanity's average height is about 5 feet. There are about 5,000 feet to a mile and, as we have observed—ten miles make the difference between the deepest ocean and the outermost mountain. That difference would be 10,000 of us standing on one another's shoulders, successively one above the other. And since in real Universe, looking at our Earth, you can't even see the altitude difference between the mountain tops and the ocean bottoms, you and I are 1/10,000 of invisible on that planet. We are indeed tiny.

We know that our planet Earth is about 1/100 the diameter of the sun. You can look at the sun when the thin cloud-cover in front of it makes it a white disc. If you take coins out of your pocket and hold them at arm's length trying to cover that disc of the sun, you'll find that a twenty-five-cent piece does just cover it neatly, and that coin is about an inch in diameter. School "rulers" are divided and marked to 1/16 inch. Engineers' scales are usually graduated to 1/50 inch, but sometimes to 1/100 inch. A hundredth of an inch is, to most human eyes, a blur. You can't really make out that difference with your eyes. Since our planet Earth's diameter is only 1/100 that of the sun, and since the disc we cover the sun with is only one inch—Earth as seen against the sun would be an almost invisible speck of 1/100 inch. Our star, sun, is a mediocre-sized star. One large star, Betelgeuse, has a diameter greater than the orbit of Earth around the sun. And our star, the sun, is only one of the 100 billion stars in our galaxy, and we now know of a billion such galaxies. I would say that when we get to that kind of knowledge about our Universe, it's clear to me that Universe affairs are not dependent upon whether the republicans or democrats are elected, nor is Universe saying we can't afford another galaxy, let alone lunch for the kids. I don't think of Universe as being concerned with the same kind of nonsense that we are. We can develop and hold a bias unreasonably. To me, Universe is something other than just stars to decorate the night.

I'd like to try to be as clear as we can about how and why we are here on this planet. Let's examine what we do know experimentally about ourselves. Let's try to analyze human beings in relation to all other living organisms, to see if we can find something different. Yes. All the other living organisms have some built-in, special equipment, part of their physical organisms, that gives them some special advantage in some special environment. There is a little vine that grows beautifully in the Amazon, but nowhere else. I see the birds have wings, so when they're in the sky they can fly, but when they're not flying, cannot take off their wings, so you see them walking awkwardly, greatly encumbered by their wings.

Human beings are not alone in having brains. Many creatures have brains. Brains are always and only coordinating the information of the senses, taking all the information coming from outside and all the information from our innards. Brains are always and only dealing with special cases. This one smells this way, this one has that temperature, so brains store memories of these *special* case packages.

But human beings also have a phenomenon—mind—and human minds have the ability, from time to time, to discover *relationships* existing *between* components of a system that are not manifest *in* any of the components, considered only separately.

Human beings, after millions of years of observing the inverted bowl of stars in the sky, see them as seemingly fixed in rememberable pattern interrelationships. But against the "bowl" of the fixed-star heavens, humans long ago successively discovered five mobile lights a little brighter, bigger, and different in color from the fixed stars, which mobile ones reappeared from time to time—sometimes singly, sometimes in company with one another. Humans in general began to recognize these mobile bright ones, and found there were five of them, which we now call "planets." Humans gave the planets the names of gods, and after a while kept records of their reappearances in relation to the moonths (months), seasons, and years. But humans kept thinking geocentrically—that is, they thought they saw the sun, moon, and stars arising from our flat, fixed world's eastern ocean, all traveling westward through our fixed sky and plunging into our western ocean. Humans needed much more instrumental development and especially mathematical capability to comprehend what is transpiring in a more realistic way: scientific, artifact-proven existence of human mathematical capabilities begins only 4,000 years ago in Babylon—when thus first manifest, mathematics are already highly sophisticated. There is a good possibility that our mathematics first developed in the Orient and gradually worked westward through India into Mesopotamia.

Three thousand years ago (that is, 1,000 years after the Babylonian mathematics' outcropping) the Greeks made magnificent additions to the geometry and algebra. Two thousand years ago the Roman Empire monopolized, quashed, and all but obliterated mathematical capability. They instituted their Roman numerals as an accounting system which could be employed by utterly illiterate servants. About 1,000 years ago, Arabs and Hindus began relaying ancient mathematical concepts via North Africa into southern Italy and Spain. In 800 A.D. al-Khwarizmi first wrote a text in Latin which introduced Arabic numerals into the Romans' Mediterranean world. But not until 1200 A.D. was al-Khwarizmi's text published. Because of the general illiteracy of those times, it took 200 years more for the concept of the cyphra (zero) and its function of positioning numbers to reach the students of northern Italy and southern Germany. Positioning of numbers (leftward or rightward) of the successive products of successive integer multipliers, written in successively lower lines, made possible both multiplication and (in reverse patterning) long division. Did you ever try to multiply or divide with Roman numerals? If you did, you found it to be impossible. When I first went to school at the beginning of the twentieth century, the older people of my world—our village pharmacist, butcher, and hardware man—asked in a friendly way whether I had as yet "learned to do my cyphers." That is how the merchants identified mathematics—as a calculating facility, to which the cypher was the key.

With the positioning of numbers, Columbus was able to develop navigational competence of a new order. Calculating capability plus telescopic observation made possible Copernicus's discovery that our Earth is a planet going around the sun with the other planets. Calculation made possible Kepler's, Galileo's and Newton's further contributions to celestial knowledge.

Mediterranean people began to use Arabic numerals as a shorthand for Roman numerals. The Roman numerals are what we call a scoring system. The masters had a servant stationed at a gate when a herd of sheep was being driven through that gate, the master said to the servant, "Every time a sheep goes by, you make a mark." That's how we got our Roman numerals.

The Arabic numerals were probably invented by ancient Arabs to copy the behavior of an abacus. An abacus has a series of vertical rods in a frame. On the rods, beads are mounted in modular groups—five below a horizontal bar and two above, for each vertical rod. You enter your progressive products and when you have all of the beads pushed up in the first column, you move one up in the next column. Thus you have a way of accumulating the products and when you *empty* the column, and you are trying to keep track of columns in Arabic numerals, you have to have a cypher to indicate an empty column.

Often losing their abacus overboard, or in the caravanning sands, the Phoenicians invented the abak, a tablet sprinkled over with sand on which they drew pictures of the rod and bead abacus array, and on which sand boards they simply entered their single symbols for the number context of the columns. They needed a symbol for an empty column, and invented the cyphra—0.

Because the Roman world was scoring and could not see or eat "no sheep," they did not comprehend or use the cyphra when they used the other Arabic numerals as shorthand symbols for their Roman numerals.

There came a series of extraordinary new situations and accomplishments now that people could calculate. Not that their intelligence was greater, but they had a facility which had to be developed cooperatively by and only between human beings that had been born, all of them naked, helpless, ignorant, driven by hunger, thirst, curiosity, lust, fear, and love, having to find their way by trial and error.

We get to an historical condition wherein calculated informations compound synergetically going back to Copernicus, Tycho Brahe, Kepler, Galileo, and Newton making much better measurements of the behaviors of those planets, and having calculating capability. Kepler found that the planets were orbiting the sun in ellipses and not in circles. Kepler also found the planets are all different in size and are operating at different distances from the sun and are all going around the sun at different rates. While they are all on the same team, they seemed otherwise to be very disorderly. Kepler, as a mathematician, then said, "I now know one thing about them: that they are all going around the sun. If I can know something else that they have in common, then I might be able to find out other at-present-unknown characteristics of their planetary system." In trigonometry, if we have two knowns, we can find out all the other characteristics of the unknowns. So Kepler said, "As a mathematician, I'm going to deliberately give them something else in common. I'm going to give them each exactly twenty-one days of time. This is much too small a time for them to demonstrate anything except a rather small arc." So, Kepler assigned twenty-one days to each, and drew a diagram of the twenty-one-day behavior for each of the planets. Each one starts at this known distance from the sun, and moves in an elliptical arc, so that at the end of the twenty-one days, the distance from the sun of each of the planets is a little bit different from its radial distance at the start. Each planet's twenty-one-day data described a thin, pie-shaped form. Kepler then said, "I might as well calculate the areas of these triangular pieces of pie. There's no pie in the sky, but I might as well calculate it." I am confident that either you or I would be mystically overwhelmed if we had been Kepler, making these calculations, and discovering that "the areas swept out by each of the planets in twenty-one days, (i.e., in exactly twenty days, twenty-three hours, fifty-nine minutes and sixty seconds) were not just approximately equal areas, but were *exactly the same.* It would be quite clear to each of us, as it was to Kepler, that, behind the superficial disorders of experience, there is some kind of elegantly exact coordinating system. This high degree of omniinterrelated cosmic coordination challenged Kepler's intellect. If the planets were touching each other like gears, then he could understand how they could coordinate. But they are multimillions of miles apart. "How can you coordinate celestial bodies at a million miles apart?" But there were other relevant facts of which Kepler knew. The first is that the planets were in elliptical orbits. "If I have a weight on a single restraint string, and swing it around my head, then its orbit will be a circle," said Kepler. "If I want to make an ellipse, I have to have two restraints. There's some type of invisible, cordless tension going on between the planets and the sun. When the planets tend to bunch together, they have a more powerful restraining effect on one another, which brings about an ellipse."

Human intellect has to imagine, as did Kepler, the existence of some incredible kinds of tendons that are absolutely invisible, that operate reliably at distances of millions and billions of miles. This conceptioning is an extraordinary challenge to the human mind. We are accustomed to pushing and pulling, but not to that kind of remote control. Kepler's knowing that there were enormous weights and enormous sizes involved to be interrestrained in such an invisible manner, made his stratagems and reasoning an extraordinary human feat.

So then we have Galileo calculating the rate of free-falling bodies, and discovering that the acceleration rate was in terms of the second power of the arithmetical distance traveled.

And then we have Isaac Newton, deeply eager to find out what Kepler's extraordinary cosmic pull might be. Newton is excited by the then-popular knowledge that human beings have identified the occurrence of very high tides of Earth's oceans with the full-moon phases. Thinking in terms of this great six quintillion tons of ocean lift, Newton realized that when we have a full moon with the sun on the same side of Earth as the moon, the sun and moon are both pulling together on Earth's oceans. The pull would be very great under those circumstances compared to other such times as when the sun and moon would be on opposite sides of Earth with the moon's minor pull cancelling some of the sun's great pull.

Isaac Newton was also greatly advantaged by the astronomers and navigators, who had, by his time, been able to catalog the angular attitudes of Earth in relation to the sun and the other planetary bodies for each day, hour, and minute of the year. So Isaac Newton then, using all the foregoing information, hypothesized his first law of motion, which said that, "A body persists in a state of rest or in a line of motion except as affected by other bodies." Newton realized that gravitational pull between the moon, Earth and sun must be enormous, in order to lift six quintillion tons several feet twice daily. He then hypothesized again that the relative initial interattraction of any two bodies in respect to that between any two other equidistanced bodies in Universe would be proportional to the product of the masses of the respective pair of bodies. The Earth-moon-sun interattractiveness is so great that the pull between two neighboring apples is overwhelmed by the pull of Earth on both of the apples. Then, Newton thought about the idea of Earth letting go of the moon, the way you can let go of a weight on a sling.

He then chose a given moment many nights hence when the moon would be in the full, and, from the astronomical data, Newton plotted the line of trajectory of the "sling-released moon" as it departed from Earth as seen against the "fixed" star bowl of the heavens and as seen from a given point on Earth. On that day and moment, Newton observed the behavior of the moon and "traveled away from that theoretical trajectory and followed the Earth," as Earth and the moon together went around the sun at 60,000 miles an hour, while the moon went around Earth, and he found the behavior of the moon exactly verified Galileo's law of "falling bodies." (We shouldn't talk about *falling* bodies, they are simply being *attracted* to other dominant bodies.) At any rate, Newton concluded that the interattractiveness of any two bodies was in terms of the second power of the mathematical distance between the bodies. If you double the distance between the two, you reduce the attraction to a quarter of what it was, if you halve the distance between the two, you increase the attraction fourfold. Newton then made this conclusion his working hypothesis, and the astronomers began to use it, and scientists since then have used it to explain all the celestial behaviors, wherever it could be appropriately employed. We have, then, Isaac Newton's discovery: what we call the gravitational law, mass attraction. If you ask Mr. Newton what "gravity" is, he would say, "There is nothing you can point to." It exists only as the interrelationship existing between bodies. There is nothing in any of the bodies *by themselves* that predicted they would be attracted to other bodies. It is only because humans for millions of years realized that the planets were, as a team, behaving seemingly differently from the rest of the stellar Universe that aroused human curiosity enough to finally discover what was going on between the members of the team that finally disclosed a cosmic law.

I want to point out that this is what human *minds* have the exclusive capability to discover—relationships existing *between,* that are not *in,* the special cases, whereas the brain is used in apprehending and remembering the special cases.

Newton's discovery is what we call a scientific generalization. To qualify as a scientific generalization means that no exceptions can be found to the operation of the principle, which means that scientific generalizations are inherently eternal. Because it deals only in special cases, all of which begin and end, the brain asks for explanations of how Universe began and is to end. But the human mind discovered that there is no beginning or ending to eternally regenerative Universe. There are only eternal principles.

Human minds have, then, the unique and exclusive capability to discover and express only mathematically, mind-discovered principles, which are some of the eternal interrelationships (principles) of Universe. All of these are synergetic. Synergy means behavior of whole systems unpredicted by the behavior of any of the system components when considered only separately.

As far as we know, only human beings have this generalized principle-discovering capability, and we have now discovered quite a family of these generalized principles. There are not so many of them that we know about, and we never know when we're going to discover one, and we don't know that the last one discovered is going to be the last one at all. But there is an at-present known family, and when we look at them sum-totally together, we learn something very fascinating: none of them has ever been found to contradict any of the others. Not only are they eternal, but they are all interaccommodative. When you and I use the word *design* in contradistinction to *chaos,* we mean that an intellect has sorted out and deliberately arranged the patterning of all the components of the experienced composition as visually, aurally, tactilely, or olfactorily apprehended in detail by the brain—but as comprehensively comprehended only by mind and expressible only as eternal interrelationship, only in mathematical terms by mind—special-case human mind discovering eternal a priori generalized mind, the intellectual concept of eternal, interaccommodative principles. It seems the human mind has limited access to the great design of Universe itself.

Human beings must have some very important function to serve in Universe, or we wouldn't be given such a cosmic capability. What we have to think about is the human's function in Universe.

I would point out to you that the most common experience of all human minds throughout history is "problems, problems, problems." In fact, if you're good at problem solving, you don't come to a problemless Utopia. You qualify for bigger and bigger problems.

Quite clearly, human beings have the capability to *discover principles* and to *employ* them. But humans can't *design* a generalized principle. For instance, they can't *design* a generalized lever. It has to be a special-case lever, made of such and such a size, and such and such material. You find, then, that human beings have the capability to *discover* principles and to employ them. For instance, we have the Wright brothers discovering how to make airplanes glide, then how to engine- and propeller-pull them into flight. Long before that, children found out how to make paper darts fly across the schoolroom. Their darts were the prototypes for the most advanced delta wing "fighters" of today. Also long ago, Bernoulli discovered the mathematically stateable law of pressure differentials in gases. Because of Bernoulli's mathematics, humans were able to calculate how to make wingfoils to give us increasing lift advantage in airplanes. And so, today, wingless human beings have made powered wings for themselves, and can fly forty-two times faster and thirteen times higher than any bird. With their diving equipment, humans can dive deeper and swim faster than a whale. In fact, humans can outperform all the specially equipped mammals in their special areas of excellence. You can take the wings and fly them, or I can fly them, or we can melt them down and make better ones as they become completely interchangeable between us. Humans have a completely different way of coping with their environment because of their minds' access to some of the principles of Universe.

The most important physical fact humans have so far learned about Universe is that no energy is being created and no energy is being lost. Universe is eternally regenerative. It is a 100 percent efficient system. In comparison, we humans make reciprocating engines which are 15 percent efficient. We make turbines which are 30 percent efficient; we make jet engines which are 60 to 65 percent efficient; we make what we call fuel cells, up to 85 percent efficient. Efficient means how much work we can get out of the energy we invest. But Universe itself is 100 percent efficient. It is the one and only completely efficient system of which we know.

For every turn to play in Universe there are six moves to be made, within twelve equioptimally economical degrees of freedom—six positive and six negative. If you want to make a wire wheel, you'll find you have to have twelve spokes; you have to have three leftward, three rightward, three backward, and three forward spokes. It takes a minimum of twelve spokes, six positive and six negative, to give you a fixed structure. In every system in our Universe that has structural stability, there are a minimum of twelve restraints. And nature always does things in the most economical manner. That is why I say that with every turn to play you have six positive and six negative, equally optimally economical alternative moves. Mathematically speaking, and from a topological viewpoint, we find that all the lines in Universe are evenly divisible by the number six. With the twelve degrees of freedom and the incredibly high frequency of event occurrences of all the different omniintertransforming systems of Universe, the frequency of turns to play is such that you can design anything—a daisy or a galaxy. One takes a little longer than the other, but all of these designs are permitted. Thus we discover our Universe to be of such extraordinary complexity that everything is everywhere transforming constantly, yet is sum-totally so intercomplementary, though nonsimultaneously, as to be 100 percent accounted, no energy being created and none being lost.

We begin to see that we have humans on board our planet to discover principles, and to employ them instrumentally, and to gain information. Just within my lifetime, we have developed such powerful telescopes and such advanced photography that we have discovered a billion galaxies. With the opening of the twentieth century, humanity has entered upon a new kind of reality. Up to the twentieth century, reality was everything we could see, smell, touch, or hear directly. When I was three years old, electrons were discovered. (I was born in 1895.) This twentieth century brought humans into electromagnetics. Within electromagnetics, we found that every chemical element has a set of unique electromagnetic frequencies which are not tunable directly by the human eye, but which can be tuned in instrumentally by what is called a spectroscope. In this century, humans have developed metallic alloys, for instance, by adding 2 percent of copper to aluminum. The aluminum becomes twice as strong in tension, but doesn't weigh any more.

In our twentieth century, we have developed a vast and ever more exquisitely effective invisible capability. In producing structures, we have evolved ever higher tensile strength with the same weight of material. We now have the ability to communicate almost weightlessly with electromagnetics. We are constantly doing more with ever less investment of physical resources per each magnitude of functional capability.

A new era of human affairs has been opened to us. In 1930, the first chart of the vast electromagnetic spectrum was published (in the United States). All the different chemical elements are present and all the radio wavelengths, the X-rays, infrareds, and then the red, orange, yellow, green, blue, violet wavelengths which you and I have the equipment to tune in directly. Then we go on into ultraviolet and further non-direct tunability of humans. We discovered that where you and I can tune in to reality is, in fact, less than one millionth of reality. All of the things that are going to affect all of our lives tomorrow are being conducted in realms of electromagnetic spectrum that can only be reached by instrument. So humanity has a very new relationship to Universe with its 99 percent invisible reality.

When we begin to think about the educational problems of humanity, we must think in terms of the whole and its inter-complementarity. We're in for a very important new phase of education wherein, as a prelude, during my lifetime, we have gone from 90 percent illiteracy of total humanity to 90 percent literacy.[38] Our little minds, probing the invisible reality, have discovered some very extraordinary principles. Human beings have been employing these principles of the invisible world, and employing them primarily in the realm of weaponry. The cost to realize use of these principles requires vast amounts of money to buy million-dollar tools. Humanity says we can't afford that. But when national defense says the enemy is going to destroy you if you don't buy these tools, our political leaders say, "All right, we have to cope with the enemy," and we bring in the highest new scientific capability in order to cope. So we have humanity employing these extraordinary principles primarily for what is called national defense. But the national defense employs scientists to discover with what the enemy is going to attack next, and this brings the most powerfully opposed political systems into escalating the forms of warfare and into exploiting realistically those highest capabilities of humanity. And then, after people have produced new weaponry, their old weapon becomes obsolete but they still have the production capabilities for it. So they look around the home front for some outlet, and so we have a gradual fallout of ever advancing technology from the military into the home front.

---

38 Literacy, as defined by the international development community, is the population, 15 and older, who can read and write. In 2005, 82 % (totaling 3.8 billion) were literate; this increased from 63 % in 1970 (totaling 1.5 billion). Of those who were *not* literate in 2005, 64 % were women. Of the 1.3 billion people *under* the age of 15, 103 million were not in primary or secondary school. UNESCO Institute for Statistics, http://www.uis.unesco.org/en/stats/statistics/literacy2000.htm (accessed September 3, 2009).

But we're operating politically on our planet according to a view first considered scientifically infallible in 1800 when Thomas Malthus, professor of political economics for East India Company College, for the first time in history had available for his study the total vital statistics from around our closed-system spherical planet. The British Empire was the first spherical empire. All the empires before were flat empires, starting with a flat-world civilization with its unknown wilderness extending laterally into infinity. If you didn't like the way things were going, you had an infinite number of chances of reaching the right god by prayer, and would come out fine. But here we have Thomas Malthus in 1800 with all the vital statistics from around the world, and he found quite clearly that humanity is multiplying itself at a geometrical rate and multiplying its life support at an arithmetical rate, wherefore humanity is clearly designed to be a failure. This concept became, then, the model of all economics and social sciences—an inherently inadequate planetary life support.

Each of the great political systems on the planet is saying, "You may not like our system, but we're convinced we have the fairest, most logical, most ingenious method of coping with an inherently inadequate life support." Because there are those who disagree completely on the method of coping, it can only be resolved by trial of arms which political system is fittest to survive. That's why, for the last thirty years, Russia and the United States have jointly spent over $200 billion a year on how to destroy most expertly,[39] rather than on how to make our world work; all on the basis that there is not enough to go around, so we don't try to use the great principles discovered by science to make the humans' world work. It was this fact, plus the new era capability to do more with the same weight, that made me resolve fifty years ago to try to reverse, and to use the high technologies only for livingry.

---

39 See note 19, p. 139.

I was an officer-of-the-line in the United States Navy in 1917, in World War I, and I found a great deal of classified information having to do with the invisible world. When, for example, you came into contact with the enemy, he knew the weight of your ship, and its tonnage, armaments, and so forth, but he did not know that your ship and its armament were made of metals that can do twice as much with the same weight as could his metals. So he was overpowered and sunk. Much of the highly classified information had to do with doing more with the same, or more with less. You don't find anything in books on economics about doing more with less. Now, it occurred to me then (way back in 1917) that if we could continue doing more with less to cope with the *enemy,* then we might someday be able to do so much with so little that we could take care of everybody peacefully. In 1927, fifty-one years ago, I committed myself to following through on that: taking the highest production capabilities of humanity and applying them to the home front. I found, at that time, that the best single-family dwelling that you could find weighed 150 tons. And I found that, using the most advanced aircraft technology and design, you could build it weighing 3 tons. I now have over 200,000 geodesic domes around the world,[40] as constant proof of producing very much more environment-controlling apparatus with ever-less amounts of physical weight of input.

We learned long ago that if you double the length of a ship, you have four times as much ship surface and eight times as much volume or payload. I learned that if I double the size of a dome, I have four times as much surface, and eight times as much volume; which means that every time I double the size of a dome, I halve the amount of surface through which an interior molecule of atmosphere can gain or lose energy as heat. This is why icebergs melt very, very slowly, but little ice cakes melt very, very fast. The smaller they get, the faster they melt. The bigger they

---

40 See note 6, p. 42.

get, the more they conserve their energy and the more energy stable they become.

So now I am able to say informedly and irrefutably that employing only humanity's proven technology and its already mined and recirculating metals, it is now clearly demonstrable that within ten years we can have all humanity living at a higher standard than anyone has heretofore experienced. During this ten-year time, we can phase out forever all further uses of nature's savings account energies—the fossil fuels, and atomic energy (nature's capital account). We can live entirely on our energy income. But I find that no one is taking that seriously.

If you get into the idea that it has to be you or me, and finally you get hold of money that makes it easier to take care of me, then you get tied up with an enormous amount of investment. The "money" does not go after low-grade ore when there is high-grade ore right next to it. Money always chooses the way which makes the most money, and in the shortest time. After it uses up the fossil fuel, it goes over to the exhaustion of atomic energy. None of the big governments or big religious organizations, and none of the private enterprises are looking seriously at using only our direct daily energy income: the three great power bureaucracies see no way of putting meters between people and the sun. I know that living entirely on our energy income is completely feasible, and I can demonstrate how it can be done. Which means that we don't have to cheat all the generations to come of their chances to survive. Which means that I now know that the working philosophy of all our major political systems is wrong, it does not have to be "only you or only me." I could not have come to this proven option until the invention of alloys demonstrated our ability to do so much with so little.

On our planet are 4 billion human beings.[41] Possibly a thousand of them know by their own experience that what I am saying

41 See note 22, p. 143.

is actually true. Ninety-nine percent of humanity does not understand science, because science is using mathematics which have no experimental evidence. Therefore 99 percent of humanity does not understand science. Ninety-nine percent does not understand that all science has ever found out is that the universe is the most incredibly reliable technology—that you and I are very much better technology than any of the machinery we have been able to design ourselves. We have the 99 percent who don't understand science thinking that technology is something new. The 99 percent connect technology only with weapons or machinery that competes for their jobs. They say, "Let's get rid of it."

All of humanity now has the option to "make it" successfully and sustainably, by virtue of our having minds, discovering principles, and being able to employ the principles to do more with less. We have that option, but humanity has been set against itself by thinking that it's against technology.

From a future educational responsibility viewpoint, nothing is more challenging than the question of how we get the 99 percent to understand technology. The universe is technology. How do we induce humanity to teach itself that a design revolution is completely different from a political revolution? The latter vengefully pulls the top down. A design revolution would elevate the bottom, and all the others, to sustainable standards of living higher than the top has ever experienced.

I've discovered that nature has a coordinate system that is completely comprehensible. She is completely four-dimensional, absolutely understandable to a child. I have elucidated this coordinate system in a book called *Synergetics,*[42] which is now in its third printing by Macmillan.

We have in the world of education a great deal of fear. The vast majority of human beings are worried about their jobs. Human beings are convinced by custom that they have to earn a living to

---

42 See note 34, p. 172.

get in on the supposedly inadequate life support. We have, then, nature trying very hard to make humans successful, but people self-frustrated by their fear.

There has been thus far a complete inability to take advantage of electronics for helping the children to educate themselves by, for example, the radio or TV cassette, where they could get their education directly from the world master of any subject such as, for instance, Einstein, instead of listening to someone who doesn't understand Einstein too well. We have our American children, now, latched on to the TV six hours a day. But they are getting nothing but poison. If we could get conceptual understanding of the mathematical coordinate system of nature on TV for those kids, we could help them to understand exactly how nature designs. The children would soon understand that they could exercise our design revolution option to make it on our planet.

Humanity has, by cosmic design wisdom, always been born helpless, naked, ignorant, hungry, thirsty, and curious, and has been forced to learn only by trial and error that our mind is everything and our muscle is nothing.

We are coming now into our final examinations, to see whether we're really going to qualify. But muscle and brain cunning are as yet in control of human affairs, not mind. If humanity omni-individually resolves to rely upon its mind, humanity could come out of this, and rebloom into a new relationship to Universe wherein people never again have to prove their right to live, that we have it automatically. The hydrogen atom does not have to earn a living before it is allowed to act like a hydrogen atom. We're about to qualify that way if we come out with mind in control.

If, in our "final exam," mind comes into control, we will exercise our option to be a physical success—all of us. The function of "Education Tomorrow" can only be exercised for about another eight years before we get to where we either have to destroy ourselves or take the option to "make it." The function of education of tomorrow is to assure that humanity qualifies to continue in Universe.

When I was young, all of humanity was remote from one another, but today, we're all integrated, we all have to act as human occupants on one spaceship planet. It has to be everybody or nobody.

Recently, nature made a drastic evolutionary move, in the following way. Amongst mammals, males cover more geography annually than females because females carry the young. Humans have acted that way, I'm sure, from the earliest time. The father was the hunter, the mother was the consolidator. Not only was Dad the hunter, but he also brought home the news. All the kids of all generations had Dad and Mom as the authority about what all the successive generations' Dads and Moms before them had said was safe to eat or do. Dad brought home the news, and told the kids about things in his own esoteric language. They listened to Dad, and, because he was the authority, they emulated his speech. This brought about more and more dialects, which in turn developed into more and more languages.

When I was thirty-two, in May 1927, all the Daddies were coming home one afternoon and the kids said, "Daddy, come in quickly. Listen to the radio. A man is flying across the Atlantic." And Dad said, "What? Wow!" and he never brought home the news again.

Nobody ever told the kids that Daddy was the authority. He was obviously so. But suddenly, in and after 1927, the kids saw Dad and Mom listening to the radio and repeating to their neighbors the radio broadcasters' news. So, quite clearly, without anyone saying so, the man on the radio was an authority greater than Dad. All the broadcasters were selected for the jobs because of the commonality of their pronunciation and because of the magnitude of their vocabulary. Because the radio broadcasters were the new authority, the children began to emulate their pronunciation and vocabulary. This is where their vocabularies came from. At the turn of the century, in my first jobs, all the workmen

I worked with had vocabularies of approximately only one hundred words, 50 percent profane or obscene. But suddenly, with the radio, came a larger, more accurate, and rich common vocabulary, everywhere around the world.

The speed of sound is 700 miles an hour. The speed of *light* is 700 million miles an hour—a million times faster than sound. Sound only works in our atmosphere—light and radiation go right on through our Universe. What humans get in the way of information visually is approximately a million times what they get by sound. In came the television. When the University of California students at Berkeley had made their first world news as dissidents, that particular group asked me to come and talk to them. The majority of them graduated in 1966. They were *born* the year the television came into the American home.

Those students said, quite clearly, "I know Dad and Mom 'love me to pieces' and I love them to pieces, but they don't know what's going on. They don't have anything to do with going to the moon, and they don't have anything to do with going to Korea." So Dad and Mom ceased to have any educational responsibility, and the kids said, "We've got to do our own thinking."

I was brought up in an era when my mother and all the teachers said, "Darling, never mind what you think, listen to what we've got to teach you." Nobody is saying that to their kids anymore. The kids suddenly found out that they had to do their own thinking, and they knew that, since we could get to the moon, we ought to be able to make our world work.

What happened here evolutionarily is similar to the case of the child within the womb. It has to have oxygen, and mother is where the oxygen is. So mother gets it into her lungs, and through her blood and the umbilical cord into the child. When the child is out of the womb, and able to get its own oxygen, we cut the cord.

Humanity is born naked, helpless, and ignorant, and has to learn by mistakes. By billions of errors, humanity has acquired much information, but the significance of the information has been frequently misinterpreted. Until Copernicus, we were the center of our Universe. We had an older world making bad explanations. Then, nature suddenly cut the metabilical cord.

Thus was created a young world in which every successive child was being born in the presence of less misinformation; every child was being born in the presence of more reliable information. Nature said. "Let's cut the 'metabilical' cord and let the young world do its own thinking."

Of course, the first such free-thinking young peoples' idealism is highly exploitable. With Russia and the United States spending $200 billion a year on getting ready for war,[43] they jointly spend about $20 billion on psycho-guerilla warfare. This is waged by breaking down the other person's economy before we get to all-out war. Thus, Russia and the United States both have pushed narcotics on the kids of the other side, and did everything they could to break down the other one's economies. The psycho-guerilla warfare succeeded in exploiting these kids at first, and then the kids discovered that the politicians had them using their heads for battering rams instead of for thinking. Very rapidly, the young developed immunities to all such political exploitation. I find the young world in love with the truth, abhorring any form of hypocrisy and superficial pretense.

I find this young world guarding and cultivating its sensitivity, and doing its own thinking, discovering great mystery. They don't need any religious teaching to recognize the incredible mystery present in life. They try to understand what, how, and why the various integrities manifest themselves in Universe.

I find the young people guarding and cultivating the phenomenon love. Love is a very extraordinary phenomenon—very mysterious.

Each child, then, is becoming successively a little less misconditioned, having a better chance to reorganize human affairs.

---

43 See note 19, p. 139.

Nature is trying very hard to make humans successful. If we *do* make it, we're going to make it by virtue of that young world and its determination to learn the truth and the synergetic inter-significance of all the truths. Once you give the young world a synergetic clue, they will find they can really understand technology and their Universe. Then, knowledge is going to proliferate very rapidly.

Because I see that we have the option to make it does not mean that I am optimistic that we will do so—I think it is absolutely touch and go as to whether we will win. I think that whether we are going to make it or not, it is really up to each one of us; it is not something we can delegate to the politicians. What kind of world are you really going to have? Are you going to really go along with experimental evidence, or just the way you were taught? Are you going to revert to letting yourself see the sun setting, the sun rising, when you know that the sun is not rising or setting? For 500 years, scientists have failed to do anything in the educational world about coordinating our senses with our knowledge. "Tomorrow's Learning" could easily teach children to see Earth revolving in respect to the sun, if you don't start their lives by saying that it is much more practical to say sun-set and sun-rise.[44] The way we're going to make it is through each one of us being thoughtfully operational about how we communicate what we know.

Seeing much of the young world all around the world, I would say there is a good chance we can make it. Spontaneously thoughtful individual integrity will be able to win, and that is exactly what the world around young individuals is beginning to manifest.

---

44 Over the years Fuller would often make this point in his writing and public speaking. Eventually he even began inviting suggestions about alternative words to "sunrise" and "sunset." He did get a number of creative responses; one suggested the alternatives *sunsight* and *sunclipse*, which he spontaneously liked and quickly adopted.

Appendix

Cover image: A sketch Bucky drew and used in his book *Critical Path* (New York, 1981) which he titled "Bird's Eye View of UN [United Nations] Geoscope." Fuller's vision for a geoscope, or as he had previously called it, a "minni-earth," was developed over many years, for "making the invisible" big pictures trends unfolding on Earth, "visible." "Minni-Earth might be suspended from masts mounted on the ring of rocks in midstream of New York City's East River, one quarter mile distant from the great east face of the United Nations building, to serve as a constant confronter of all nations' representatives of the integrating patterns, both expected and unexpected, occurring around the face of man's constantly shrinking 'one-town world.'" *Ideas and Integrities* (Baden, 2010), p. 343. See also p. 73 in this volume.

DOME CLIMBING

CHILD'S INATE COORDINATION - SUBJECTIVE.
- INTERNAL
- EXTERNAL
- INTERMITTENT
- OMNI DIRECTIONAL.

CHILDREN'S PICTURES COORDINATE COMMUNICATION
HOUSE, TREES, BIRDS, SUN & MOON ~~TOGETHER~~
CHILDREN RIGHT & DYNAMICLY SYNCHRONOUS
PARENTS WRONG STATIC, LOCAL. ONE STILL PICTURE

RELTE
MORLEY'S POEM.

I came upon a very interesting manuscript in the Fuller Archive at Stanford, called "Dome Climbing," with a lot of Bucky's handwritten pages. The spirit of the text seemed so fitting for this volume on education. It also piqued my interest, bringing to mind an early memory of climbing a small jungle-gym dome, which Bucky had installed in our backyard, at the age of five with my sister Alexandra. One such experience was memorialized in my father Robert Snyder's first documentary film on Bucky called *Sketchbook*. As I flipped through the manuscript file, it looked

The children coordinate spontaneously -- internally (organically) as well as externally in body balance and articulation. Their experiences are inherently omni-directionally oriented. Their heads point in succession of star directions and their experience patternings are inherently intermittent. Go to sleep -- forget -- change focus -- continual change of observer position in universe, physically and mentally.

HIERARCHY OF MICRO - MACRO

ASTRO globe.

World globe (note shape of No. America)

World Map - Fuller (Note shape of No. America)

Map of America (Seen now in greater detail)

Map of United States

Map of California

Map of Los Angeles

Your House

PAIN IN TUMMY.

You - part of you -- your hand, a finger, a finger nail. Inside you. Invisible you.

a little uncharacteristically like a sketch for some extemporaneous comments, like a film script. And then I noticed some handwriting that looked like my father's. Could it be? And then, sure enough, I found an old manila envelope folder tab with the words: "'Dome Climbing' BF Text for Time Inc 'Scrapbook' Nov. 4." Time Inc. funded my father's project proposal: a first "magazine of the arts," which also included short films of Willem de Kooning and Igor Stravinsky. (R. Buckminster Fuller Archive, Special Collections, Stanford University)

EDUCATION AUTOMATION:

Freeing the scholar to return to his studies

A Discourse before the Southern Illinois University

Edwardsville Campus Planning Committee,

April 22, 1961

by R. BUCKMINSTER FULLER

Foreword by CHARLES TENNEY

SOUTHERN ILLINOIS UNIVERSITY PRESS

CARBONDALE, ILLINOIS

Title page of final page proofs of the first edition of *Education Automation,* published in 1962 while Bucky was Professor at Southern Illinois University, which, in its entirety, became chapter 2 of *R. Buckminster Fuller On Education* as well as this edition.
(R. Buckminster Fuller Archive, Special Collections, Stanford University)

Resources

The Buckminster Fuller Institute
www.bfi.org
Founded in 1983, The Buckminster Fuller Institute serves a global network of design science innovators working at the leading edge of the design revolution Fuller inspired—including the Buckminster Fuller Challenge, an annual $100,000 prize to support the development and implementation of solutions to humanity's most pressing problems.
181 N. 11th St., Suite 402/Brooklyn, NY 11211/718 290-9280

The R. Buckminster Fuller Archive
www-sul.stanford.edu/depts/spc/fuller/index.html
Called in 1976 by archivists from the Smithsonian Institute, "the most extensive personal archive in existence," the collection contains over 1,300 linear feet of papers and manuscripts, 2,000 hours of video and audio recordings, and thousands of models and other artifacts.
Dept. of Special Collections/The Stanford University Libraries/Stanford, CA 94305

The Estate of R. Buckminster Fuller
www.buckminsterfuller.net
Fostering the preservation, publication, and dissemination of Buckminster Fuller's legacy.
P.O. Box 3248/Santa Barbara, CA 93130/Fax: 805 456-2912

The Earth Policy Institute
www.earthpolicy.org
The Earth Policy Institute, dedicated to building a sustainable future as well as providing a plan of how to get from here to there, publishes the remarkable book *Plan B 3.0: Mobilizing to Save Civilization* by founder and President Lester R. Brown (free online access).
1350 Connecticut Ave. NW, Suite 403/Washington, DC 20036/Fax: 202 496-9325

The ONE Campaign
www.one.org
The *campaign to make poverty history* is over 2.4 million people committed to raising public awareness about the issues of global poverty, hunger, disease, and efforts to fight such problems in the world's poorest countries.

Rocky Mountain Institute
www.rmi.org
An independent, entrepreneurial, nonprofit organization fostering the efficient and restorative use of resources to make the world secure, just, prosperous, and life-sustaining, co-founded by scientist Amory Lovins, and featuring publications such as their groundbreaking *Winning the Oil Endgame: Innovation for Profits, Jobs, and Security* (free online access).
2317 Snowmass Creek Road/Snowmass, CO 81654/970 927-3851

The We Campaign
www.wecansolveit.org
A project of The Alliance for Climate Protection—a nonprofit, nonpartisan effort founded by Nobel laureate and former Vice President Al Gore that aims to halt global warming through educating people in the U.S. and around the world that the climate crisis is both urgent and solvable.

Bibliography

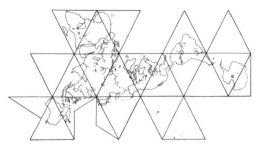

Fuller Projection World Map, 1938, 1954

Books by R. Buckminster Fuller
4-D Timelock, 1928
Nine Chains to the Moon, 1938
Education Automation, 1962
Untitled Epic Poem on the History of Industrialization, 1962
Ideas and Integrities, 1963
No More Secondhand God, 1963
World Design Science Decade,[1] 1963–1967
Operating Manual for Spaceship Earth, 1969
Utopia or Oblivion: The Prospects for Humanity, 1969
Buckminster Fuller to the Children of the Earth, 1972
Intuition, 1972
Earth, Inc., 1973
Synergetics: Explorations in the Geometry of Thinking,[2] 1975
Tetrascroll, 1975
And It Came to Pass—Not to Stay, 1976
On Education,[3] 1979
Synergetics 2: Further Explorations in the Geometry of Thinking,[2] 1979
Critical Path,[4] 1981
Grunch of Giants, 1983
Inventions: The Patented Works of R. Buckminster Fuller, 1983
Cosmography: A Posthumous Scenario for the Future of Humanity,[4] 1992

Published by Lars Müller Publishers
Ideas and Integrities: A Spontaneous Autobiographical Disclosure, new edition 2010
Education Automation: Comprehensive Learning for Emergent Humanity, new edition 2010
And It Came to Pass—Not to Stay, new edition 2008
Operating Manual for Spaceship Earth, new edition 2008
Utopia or Oblivion: The Prospects for Humanity, new edition 2008
*Fuller Houses: R. Buckminster Fuller's Dymaxion Dwellings and
    other Domestic Adventures*, Federico Neder, 2008
Your Private Sky: The Art of Design Science, Volume 1, 1999,
    edited by Joachim Krause and Claude Lichtenstein
Your Private Sky: Discourse; The Art of Design Science, Volume 2, 2000,
    edited by Joachim Krause and Claude Lichtenstein

1   With John McHale
2   In Collaboration with E. J. Applewhite
3   Robert D. Kahn and Peter H. Wagschal, editors
4   Kiyoshi Kuromiya, Adjuvant